the messenger
Denise Lescano, Psychic Medium

PUBLISHING

the messenger
Copyright © 2010 Denise Lescano
ISBN 978-0-9884562-0-4

www.deniselescano.com

Page Design by: Chad Lilly
Cover Design by: Denise Lescano and Chad Lilly

All Rights reserved. No part of this book may be reproduced in any form or by electronic or mechanical means, including information storage and retrieval systems, without permission in writing from the publisher, except by a reviewer who may quote a brief passage in a review.

www.spiritworkspublishing.com

Based on and inspired by all true stories
  – including my own.

Acknowledgments

This book is dedicated to: all of the people and spirits who have inspired this story through their lives and deaths, and who have touched my life in profound and unforgettable ways. Thank you for allowing me to peek into the spirit side of life. I am forever honored and humbled to share your stories and to be a part of such a miraculous experience.

My husband Javier who believed me, and has always believed in me, and who has taught me that it is ok to just be me.

My son Chris, who came into my life to heal my broken heart and fill my life with love and joy. I am so proud of you, and I'm proud to be your Mom!

My most beloved and spoiled dog, Sage who kept me company many late nights while writing this book.

I have to give a very special thanks to Jane Heady, Bob Riley and Jerry Eddleman for believing in me, seeing the value of my work as a way to help others, supporting me and lending me their credibility and good name. Without them, the groundbreaking support group work would not have been possible.

Special Thanks and gratitude to author, Stacy D. Shelton for all of her help, including editing the manuscript

In loving memory of "Nick" who inspired this book in ways that only he and I will ever know.

To Alan Arcieri, my dear friend and mentor, who was not here long enough, but did so much with the time he had. You were a great teacher and inspiration to so many, including me. Thank you for everything; I am eternally grateful for your generosity, unfailing support and I am honored by your friendship.

My dear friend Lindsey who has been my loyal friend since childhood and through it all.

My Grandmother Sue, Grandfather Kesner and Aunt Trish who taught me the meaning of unconditional love and family values. You have always loved, encouraged and supported me – just as I am. Thank you for all of your love and support.

And for my Mom.

Table of Contents

9	Foreword
19	Preface
23	Chapter 1: The Beginning - As it was 1984
35	Chapter 2: Passion and Discovery
41	Chapter 3: Surprises and Beautiful Music
47	Chapter 4: The Beginning of The End
55	Chapter 5: Love My Way, It's a New Day…
65	Chapter 6: A New Beginning
81	Chapter 7: Happiness Is No Tan Lines & A Tropical Tan
93	Chapter 8: Revolution, Chaos & Revelation - In That Order
105	Chapter 9: Fear of Spiders
113	Chapter 10: The Spirit Side of Life: The Coma
123	Chapter 11: Break on Through to The Other Side
137	Chapter 12: The Great Mystery
147	Chapter 13: Virtual Reunions
153	Chapter 14: Ghosts of my Boyfriend Past
165	Chapter 15: A Haunting Message
177	Chapter 16: The "Grateful" Dead
187	Chapter 17: The Messenger

Foreword

I have been fortunate that part of my work since 2005 has involved helping others who have lost loved ones through sudden and accidental deaths and suicide, as well as those, struggling with addiction. Part of that fortune has come from being able to work with three amazing counselors in this groundbreaking work. Together, it has been our collective goal and mission to open minds, challenge assumptions and in doing so, give people in need of healing and answers, some peace and clarity.

Each one of these counselors has twenty years of experience in their field of specialty, and although people may always question my validity and credibility, no one could ever question theirs. All three have committed their lives and volunteered countless hours to tirelessly helping others. While we worked together, Jane Heady, who's now retired, facilitated the Grief Support Group for Sudden and Accidental Death and also worked as the Victim's Advocate for the local State Attorney's Office. Bob Riley facilitates the Suicide Support Group and Jerry Eddleman facilitates a Twelve Step Group, where I currently work. Over the years, I have also worked with several other grief groups, as well as, a chapter of Over Eaters Anonymous.

I have been doing this long enough to know that most people want "proof" that I am real and can actually do what I claim. And, because not everyone who reads this book, will or can, have a reading with me, I am honored that these three individuals have and continue to support me. Here is what they have to say:

> I am retired now, but for twenty years, I worked as a Victim Advocate/Grief Counselor for Mothers Against Drunk Driving and for a Crisis Center in Southwest Florida. The clients who came to us for help had lost loved ones due to sudden, tragic death, such as suicide, car crashes, over doses, etc.
>
> During my years as a grief counselor for the crisis center in Florida, I had heard many "stories" from my clients about their experiences with mediums. I had never personally had occasion to see a medium and was never quite sure, if in fact

connecting with loved ones who had gone before us, was even possible!

When a client told me that a medium they had seen privately, by the name of Denise Lescano, had offered to do group sessions for our crisis center, I was a bit skeptical. But, after careful consideration I hesitantly agreed to facilitate the meetings. In the back of my mind, I kept telling myself that it was for the good of my clients – it was what they wanted. I had done some research years before on mystical experiences and looking back on my own life experiences, I thought that there might be some truth to connecting with those who have gone before us. However, I was not prepared for what was to come.

I remember vividly, the first session with Denise. I think that there were eight people present that night. The day before the meeting I only told her how many were going to attend. She did not know names or the circumstances of the death of their loved ones. I told her NOTHING. When the session began, I was immediately blown away by what I was witnessing. I knew that the readings were true connections from beyond, because there was no way she could know any of the things that were being revealed. I knew these facts to be true because these were clients who had been coming to me for individual sessions and we had talked about these things.

There are so many stories I could tell you from all of the sessions, but a few stand out in my mind. I was counseling a grandmother who was raising her 10-year-old grandson after his mother was hit by a car while she was walking. During one session his mother came through and said that she was with him always – she said that she was with him in art class that day and told in detail what he was drawing! She described his bedroom, even down to the glow in the dark stars she had put on his ceiling for him before she died. She told him that she tucks him in bed and that she kisses him each night before he goes to sleep. Can you imagine what that meant to that little boy? Then there was the teenage boy who had died of suicide who told his Mom, "I am so happy that you are wearing my necklace." She stood up and pulled the chain out from her blouse in amazement. No one could even see that she had a necklace on! He went on to tell her that he was safe and no longer in pain. Imagine how, that alone, helped her to heal. I vividly remember the spirit of a 24- year-old man who had died of a drug overdose. He kept telling his brother that he was worried about him and that he could see he was going down the same road. Two years later, I learned that the brother had also died of an overdose. When I called Denise to tell her she said that she knew because both boys had come to her that day when she was at home!

Over the next two years, faithfully each month, Denise did group readings for the clients of the crisis center. It was a gift beyond words to those who were in great pain. During the sessions, I would try to write down everything that the spirits were saying to their loved ones and many people carried those notes with them everywhere they went! I saw what a great comfort it was to them and how it helped tremendously with the healing process.

Denise had nothing to gain from these sessions, as she volunteered her time. Words can never express what it meant to those who were hurting. Denise Lescano is one in a million and I am privileged to call her "friend."

Jane Heady, Grief Counselor/Victim Advocate,
Collier County State Attorney's Office-retired

An ancient Roman philosopher, Lucius Annaeus Seneca, once said, "Luck is what happens when preparation meets opportunity." With no forethought of my own, my earlier life experiences had prepared me for an opportunity that appeared a few years ago when I met Denise Lescano.

Although she says that she never had a penchant for drugs or alcohol in excess, such is not the case with many of us. According to a recent study conducted by the National Institutes of Alcohol Abuse and Alcoholism, 8.5 percent of adults in the United States meet the criteria for alcoholism, and another two percent meet the criteria for drug addiction.

In other words, at least one in every ten Americans has a serious problem with drugs or alcohol. According to the Substance Abuse and Mental Health Services Administration (SAMHSA), five million U.S. citizens attended self-help meetings for drug and alcohol related issues, and about one-third of those people attended some form of inpatient or outpatient treatment last year. When considering the impact that alcoholism and drug addiction have on family members, co-workers, neighbors, employers, and health care providers, almost no one escapes completely unscathed. Clearly, these are problems of universal proportions that are affecting the entire human race.

The disease of alcoholism took me on a twenty-two year roller coaster ride from my early teens through my early thirties and left a trail of wreckage that has taken decades to repair. For the past twenty years, I have worked diligently, as a layperson, to be of some helpful service to others who are struggling to overcome their addictions. Ever since we began to recognize alcoholism and addictions as treatable illnesses, we've made great strides in the areas of medicine, science, and psychology that have contributed significantly to the rehabilitation of millions of people. However, even the most advanced therapies can only go so far, and, in spite of our best efforts, long-term recovery rates are abysmally small.

Successful rehabilitation takes place at physical, mental, and psychological levels. But, we often fail to address another vital aspect of recovery. The critical missing element is "spiritual." The eminent Swiss psychiatrist, Dr. Carl Jung, wrote:

You see, "alcohol" in Latin is "spiritus" and you use the same word for the highest religious experience as well as for the most depraving poison. The helpful formula therefore is: *spiritus contra spiritum*.

Experience with the realm of the spirit may be essential to the process of overcoming addictions. Recovery from alcoholism and other addictive disorders is a complex, dynamic process, and in this effort we should not hesitate to use every available tool. Therefore, when I became aware that Denise Lescano was interested in using her psychic gifts to help people to more fully recover from drug addiction and alcoholism, I contacted several friends, and we began to work with her. Our early efforts in recovery were a necessary preparation for what we later learned from Denise. She brought us important messages from "the other side" of life, and we connected to spirit guides who helped us to focus on areas that we needed to work on. For some, it was about healing past trauma or getting honest about current life situations or challenges. She told others about the precise things they needed to do to take better care of their health through dietary and exercise changes. Denise painstakingly addressed each person's particular recovery needs.

Over the years I have worked with hundreds of people in recovery, and I have learned firsthand what the attrition rates are like. A full fifty percent of those making an initial attempt at sobriety will not still be sober ninety days later, and many more drop by the wayside over the next few months. By the end of the first year, with perhaps a single exception, every graduate of a twenty-eight day treatment program will have relapsed. I know because I was such an exception, and twenty years later the statistics have not improved. Most people simply do not recover, and those of us who do remain abstinent, continue to defy the odds on a day-to-day basis.

Initially, I contacted about a dozen men and women that I knew in recovery to see who might be willing to participate in "gallery" type readings with Denise. Interestingly, none of my male friends have thus far been willing (I expect that to change shortly). However, eight women have volunteered to come at various times. Some have visited with Denise on two or more occasions, and some only attended a single session. They represented various lengths of sobriety ranging from six months to over thirty years, with an average of nine to ten years of recovery. Seven of the eight have remained continuously clean and sober during this two year period, and one who relapsed on pain medication is now back in recovery.

Do I think that Denise's talent for bringing information through from the spirit side of life was totally responsible for this statistical miracle? No, not totally. There were many other factors to consider. However, I am entirely satisfied that the information presented to each individual contributed significantly to their self-awareness and gave them additional insights and tools to assist them and enhance the quality of their recoveries.

Typically, Denise would offer certain knowledge that "validated" the information being received. For example, she provided C.H. with insights that assured her that she was indeed in contact with her deceased husband. Once that was accomplished, she was given information that was specifically addressed to her, such as the fact that the co-dependency and enabling patterns that she was experiencing with her step-son, were mirroring the same issues that she had previously encountered with her late husband, and, if she didn't get a handle on those issues, they could possibly lead her into relapse. He also assured her that he would be assisting her from spirit and that it would be essential for her to stay closely involved with her recovery groups if she was to remain sober. Finally, he tried to encourage her to not give up "before the miracle happens."

Similarly, Denise gave C.O. validating information from her deceased mother regarding the rabbits her mother had given to her when she was still in the physical body. Once the validation was accepted, her mother went on to discuss a life-threatening illness that C.O. was battling. Her mother told her that the cancer she was currently receiving treatment for was a big part of the cleansing and purging processes that were necessary for her to be able to release her addictions, and other issues, in this lifetime.

M.L.'s maternal grandmother discussed with her the details of the recent traumatic break-up of a romantic relationship and then talked specifically about her recovery from alcohol and drug addiction. Her grandmother assured her that she had successfully overcome the larger issues of her addictive behaviors and that all that would be necessary for her to maintain her sobriety would be for her to "stick with the program."

Denise brought forth specific validating information for each individual in attempts to enhance their recovery efforts. Not once did she offer generic platitudes or repeat information from one person to the next. She provided each person with exactly what they specifically needed to hear that would be of maximum benefit to them as individuals. This was the most therapeutic "counseling" that I have ever witnessed. There was catharsis, healing, and hope for everyone who joined us in these sessions.

Undoubtedly, some will dismiss the possibility of this kind of spiritual assistance; if I hadn't seen it and benefited from it personally, I might have been one of them. But, to those who may be open to it, I see this as pioneering work with the possibility of greatly enhancing our understanding of the root causes and conditions surrounding the diseases of addiction. It may also increase the probability of many additional recoveries from destructive habits and disorders. No one has ever attempted to use spirit communication to enhance recovery from alcoholism and drug addiction before, and it is exciting to witness these ground-breaking discoveries in rehabilitation. A friend of mine likes to say, "The mind is like a parachute in that it only works when it's open." To that I would add Joseph Dunninger's comment that: "For those who believe, no explanation is necessary; for those who do not, no explanation will suffice."

I consider myself fortunate indeed to be able to share this unique opportunity with someone that, unbeknownst to me, I was previously prepared to work with.

Very truly yours,

Jerry D. Eddleman, Founder and President
The Serenity Club of Naples, Twelve Step Groups

It has been said that all of life is our teacher and we are forever in a classroom. That makes so much sense as we definitely are on a journey in each of our lives. Along the way, my travels crossed paths with a very caring, compassionate and intuitive woman named Denise Lescano. A psychic medium with incredible talents and abilities, she has continuously shown this grief and life coach what a professional medium is about. Over the last five years, Denise has demonstrated to me what character, integrity, respect, compassion and sincerity is with a medium who genuinely owns these accolades. I was very honored to have been given this opportunity to describe Denise and her wonderful talents to you.

Being a professional coach who works with people in helping to build their life and assist ones in grief, my focus is on having a no nonsense approach. This is exactly what had impressed me so much about the work Denise does. My observations over the years have been one of absolute pinpoint accuracy she brings to her clients. I have sat with many, many clients through these past 5 years and the work Denise has done with our survivors group is that of "par excel lance." I have been involved with co-facilitating a survivors group for individuals who have lost someone to suicide. We have been meeting weekly for close to 23 years presently and Denise's contribution to our members grief walk is beyond compare and unparalleled.

Denise has been tested professionally for being legitimate, which has been very important to her work and reputation. The effects and results generated from her work, that I have observed, are indeed quite phenomenal. I know too well the stories and heartaches our members live with. Denise has never been made aware of any knowledge about whom she reads for. When she confronts them with factual truth, they know in that moment, she has delivered very succinct, personalized information, which comes from spirit. Denise has what she refers to as "spiritual integrity" which means she is giving the clients exactly what Spirit is sending without being filtered. I have myself experienced a personal reading with Denise and she was right on the mark. To the skeptics, I say you have the absolute right to your opinion. It is unfortunate with that outlook you will never experience the quality of a connection with a loved one's spirit that Denise provides.

The lives of our members have been so enriched and nurtured as a result of Denise's readings. They have discovered very essential information that was lacking since the death of their loved one. So much peace, closure and resolve have been given to so many of our clients. Some messages deal with future events for people to grow into and yet a number of times Spirit will bring through situations and information which has taken place, well after the time of their death.

One isolated reading we had was with a son who was on the other side. He was doing his best to persuade his mom that the reading was real and true, by describing his grandmother's suicide attempt. He described her lying on a bathroom floor, in a pool of blood after cutting her wrists. He was working really hard, as was Denise, to convince his mother that he and his grandma were there, wanting to connect with her. It took her some time to remember the incident, but when she finally did it provided the proof she needed that the experience was real. It was the catalyst which caused a sudden breakthrough in her healing process.

So many lives have been given the glow of satisfaction, validation, love, kinship, awareness and overall spiritual guidance through the genuineness of Denise's psychic expertise. She is superb – the real deal and believe me when I tell you, I willingly place my lifelong reputation on the line in validating her true psychic abilities.

I would like to present to you her story about the trials and tribulations of a psychic's life journey. I am both humbled and proud to call this fine, talented, gifted and genuine person, psychic medium, Denise Lescano, my dear friend.

Bob Riley, Professional Grief and Life Coach
Facilitator of the Group "SAS" - Surviving After Suicide
www.BobRileyCoaching.com

Preface

I have struggled for awhile with the question of whether to write this book as "my story" or just a story about all fictional characters. But, I came to the conclusion, that my story is so unusual and unique that it would be best to write it with my own words and from my point of view. I also felt that to know that this story – that all of these stories – are actually "true stories," will make the impact of these words have more significance and meaning for the reader. This is a story of hope and love, and the people who inspired this story show us that there is love and hope in the midst of even the greatest tragedy. They will show you that there is no greater force than love and it transcends and truly conquers everything including death. More importantly, my story is also the story of so many others who have touched my life profoundly, and I believe to give their stories the tribute that they deserve, I must tell them as they are – as true stories. So to tell you my story, I must also tell you their stories, because without theirs, mine would not be much of a story.

I must ask you to understand as you read this book, that all of the stories you are about to read, including my own are true. Please also understand that in an effort to respect these families, people and spirits who have inspired this story, all of the names, events and details of events have been changed. Many characters and stories may actually be the culmination of several stories and I have taken "Creative License" in writing these stories to protect the privacy, confidentiality and the sensitivity of the families and stories involved. In doing so, I have done my very best to present their loved ones' messages and legacies as accurately and truthfully as possible. It is my hope that as the people who inspired this story read my words from this side and the other, they will know I have compassionately and respectfully captured the essence of the life and legacy they left behind.

I have not written this story alone and have had the help of the many spirits who have inspired it. They asked me to pass along this message:

"That it is true, that the only thing you have to fear in this life and the afterlife is fear itself and that once you have conquered that you are truly free." They also say: *"That it is not important how much time we have here, whether our lives are short or long, but what is important, is what we did with the time we had."*

I hope that their stories touch your heart as much as they have mine and that through this work, you may understand just a little more of what your own story is really all about.

Chapter 1
The Beginning - As it was 1984

The Beginning - As it was 1984

The clock radio goes off waking me to the high pitched voice of Cindi Lauper chirping "oohhh, Girls just wanna have fun, that's all they really waaant...."

It's 7:00am and freezing in the attic where my new bedroom is located. No matter what time I go to bed, or how long I sleep I will always, as long as I live, hate being awoken by the alarm. I am just not a morning person. It just seems unnatural to be awakened abruptly in the midst of a deep sleep. To add insult to injury, I also hate winter, and for that matter, school too. I roll on to my back and look over to my second-story window, to see that it is still dark outside, at least as much as I can tell through the ice that has formed on the inside and outside of the windows. Winter in Baltimore is a depressing place to be as far as I'm concerned. It is not really cold enough to snow much, which might actually be fun. It is just cold enough to be miserable, as it rains from about November to March. The temperatures generally hang out in the 30's to 40's most days. But, the part that really makes it a depressing place to be – the absolute worst part – is the overwhelming lack of sunshine. It is the main reason I find getting up in the mornings so difficult.

Why is school so early? How can anyone expect a kid to get up while it is still dark outside and be awake and ready to learn? To me that is not getting up in the morning, that is getting up in the middle of the night! I hit the snooze button and roll back over, close my eyes and drift back to sleep.

"This is Weasel and you are listening to WHFS 99.5…time to wake up Baltimore! Next up brand new U2, *Sunday Bloody Sundaaay…*" the alarm clock radio squawks once again. I open my eyes…*Shit!* It's 7:20 and I'm going to be late for the bus again. The attic is freezing in the winter regardless of how high the heat is on. Because of this, I generally sleep in sweats with at least three blankets. This makes getting out of bed in the morning all the more difficult.

Shortly after my Mom married Francis, we moved into the small two story painted brick house in Towson. There are two bedrooms downstairs and two make-shift bedrooms, which were added later, in the attic. The previous owners had never really finished them. The walls on the second floor are only partially covered with a grey-blue wood paneling, leaving bare patches throughout, where the wood framework and insulation are exposed. There is one single door at the bottom of the stairs which is the entrance to the attic. It opens from the main living room and as you walk up to the top of the stairs into the attic, there is a bathroom straight in front with a bedroom on each side both without doors.

I guess my parents bought the house with the intention of finishing the work – as a fixer upper – but to this day still never have. In an effort to keep my bedroom warm, I've hung a sheet over the doorway to my bedroom and installed a portable plug-in heater. It doesn't do much but it helps a little.

I hate the attic but I do like the privacy. My mom had offered it to me when we moved in, because she said she thought I would like the privacy, seeing as how now I am a teenager and all. However, I have always felt that the real reason I was "offered" the attic was so that she and Francis could have *their* privacy. After all, they were newlyweds when we moved in. So, my feelings about my room in the attic fall into a love-hate category at this point, I hate the cold in winter and the stifling heat in summer but I do like my privacy.

Still half asleep, I force myself out of the warmth of my bed and into the frosty dry air. I make my way to the bathroom, which is also part of my love hate relationship with the attic. The bathroom gives me the creeps and is a constant source of fear and anxiety for me. In fact, it is the backdrop for many of my nightmares. It is located in the very back corner of the attic and must have been the last thing added to the addition. It was still in the rough and unfinished stages of construction when we moved in. The walls are framed with 2x4's and filled with insulation but are unfinished and exposed.

the messenger

The drywall and finish work was never completed. It has one very small window which is located directly in front of a large tree, on the north side of the house, allowing little light to come through. There is no shower or bath, only a toilet and small sink. There is one bare light bulb located just above the sink and a dark empty space at the opposite end of the bathroom which I imagine is where the tub is supposed to be and is not. It is always dark and gloomy, especially at the far end, and without question, it is the coldest room in the house. The toilet seat is torturous to sit on in the morning. Plus, I have to turn the sink on full blast, letting the water run at least five minutes before it turns from ice cold to tepid. But, these things alone are not the source of my nightmares about the bathroom.

I am not afraid of most things. In fact my friends and family would probably say, much to my mother's dismay, that I am pretty fearless and possibly a bit impetuous. However, I am absolutely and irrationally terrified of spiders. I hate them. I hate the way they look, their webs, all of their eyes – everything about them. They are totally gross and they give me the creeps. And, as much as I hate spiders, I hate their webs. The feeling of accidentally sticking my hand into, or walking into a spider web, can send me into an absolute hysterical tirade. I know the fear is irrational and it is hard for me to understand it but I have no idea where it comes from. All I know, is the bathroom is full of spiders and webs. They are every where – in the corners of the ceiling, between the wood frame work, under the sink and behind the toilet. Every now and then I get brave enough to go in with a can of bug spray and a broom and knock them all down, only to find that a few days later, their brothers and sisters and cousins have moved back in. It has been a never ending battle and the creepy little invaders are winning. I do not have nightmares often, but occasionally when I do they are not about ghosts, murderers or monsters, they are about spiders. So you can see why I have such a terrible time coping with my bathroom in the attic.

I barely have enough time to get ready before I'm going to miss the bus. Looking in the mirror, I think to myself that I hate my hair. It is long and blonde, but very fine and in the winter, it's just a staticy and stringy mess. I hate how flat it looks, but I have no time today to tease it and make it big, so I think I'll just stick it in a banana clip and go. It is supposed to be in the low 30's today, so I throw on a pair of purple acid washed jeans, a long sleeved t-shirt, black sweat shirt, my black converse high-tops and my hot pink leather jacket. I don't like to feel cold and I know that I will not be warm enough in my pink leather jacket, but fashion is more important than comfort, so I'll suck it up and wear it anyway. The black knit fingerless gloves do not do much good either but they do match my scarf.

The first floor is much warmer than the attic and I can feel the warmth immediately as I open the door at the bottom of the stairs. Francis is at the kitchen table reading the paper and having coffee. He is a laidback, rather relaxed man of few words. He doesn't really acknowledge me as I sit at the table and prepare to dig into a bowl of Lucky Charms. He continues sipping his coffee and reading the paper without looking up or saying a word. The news is on the TV in the next room, and I can hear President Reagan's words being analyzed and dissected by two television news guys.

My mom enters the kitchen, rushing around in her usual stressed manner. She is issuing orders to Francis and me and multi-tasking as she prepares coffee and her papers for her 9:00 client. My Mom works part time now as a bookkeeper. She is a very attractive woman with blonde hair, a petite frame and a beautifully sculpted face with high cheekbones and deep-set green eyes. She is the type of women that is always noticed when she walks into a room, by women and men alike. She's a real looker, as they say. She divorced my dad when I was only two or three, I think, and we have not seen much of him since.

My dad is a rather complicated story. I don't know too much about him really and have only met him just a few times, but not until about a year ago when I started high school. No one in the family will talk too much about him. When I was about 13-years-old, I became more and more curious about him. I wanted to know where he was, what happened to him and why I never heard from him or saw him. So, my mom and grandmother decided to sit me down and tell me the real story about my father.

They told me that he had spent the past nine years in a state run mental health hospital for the criminally insane. They pulled out an old yellowed newspaper clipping about him and showed me. He had been diagnosed as a schizophrenic. It was clear to me that my mother was afraid of him and had done everything in her power to keep me away from him. They told me that he had a history of hearing voices and delusional behavior.

The Baltimore Sun article spoke of some experimental treatment that was being used on him to control the voices and delusions. I was also told that he would be getting out soon and that I was not to see him if he contacted me, unless it was with supervision. Wow! That was pretty scary and not the story I had expected to hear at all.

the messenger

Life had not been easy for mom and me when it was just the two of us. She was very young, only twenty-one when I was born. We had our struggles over the years and I know she is happy to be married to Francis now and have the pressure off a bit. However, she is just wound so tight all the time it is not always easy to live with her. She doesn't seem to know how to relax and always seems to be stressed or worrying about something.

Francis, on the other hand, is just the opposite and has a calm temperament and a laidback demeanor. He used to have a good sense of humor, but as time and life have gone on, I've noticed that his sense of humor has faded and comes out less and less. He is mostly quiet and serious these days.

The bus stop is on the corner, only three houses down, but the walk is unbearable. It is cold and windy with freezing rain and although the sky is beginning to brighten, it is still dark, grey and gloomy. I think to myself how much I hate to be cold. My face feels like it is going to crack and my hair is beginning to get coated with a thin layer of ice. I can hear the tapping of the rain against my leather jacket and the dampness and cold is piercing and penetrating right through my jeans. I'm in my junior year and most of the kids at the bus stop are younger than me, except for Kathy and Todd Baker. Kathy has been in my classes since junior high. She is wearing her usual faded blue jeans, brown leather jacket and brown suede Wallaby's. She smokes and is puffing away on her Marlboro Lights cigarette, which she only buys in the box and which she has already become addicted too. What started out as an earlier act of rebellion has now formed into a full-fledged habit. I am so happy I never started smoking and think to myself how much I hate the smell.

Todd and I have been friends for a very long time. He is one year older than me and a Senior now. He lives a few blocks away and we have hung around together in some of the same social circles in the neighborhood over the years. Todd is a really funny guy and I consider him to be one of my best friends. He is good natured, always in a good mood and up for any sort of adventure that I might cook up. He also has a car – a van actually – which makes getting to the adventures much more fun. Todd and I are just friends, but we are quite inseparable most of the time. He shares my love of punk rock music and has gone with me all over Baltimore to some of the seediest corners of downtown so we could watch the latest Punk band play in what is usually some sort of abandoned warehouse. We have seen the

Ramones together 3 times. He is of average height, but on the taller side, with blonde wavy hair and blue eyes. He always has rosy cheeks and lips and a big smile. Whenever he comes to pick me up, my mother asks why he wears two different colored shoes. He always wears one red and one blue converse high top. It's a statement. I'm not sure what it's saying, but it is a statement, none the less.

The bus pulls up to the corner of York Road and Cavan Drive with its lights still on and its brakes' squeaking as it finally comes to a stop. We file on and I sit down next to Kathy, who now smells like a mixture of Wella Balsam Shampoo, Marlboro Cigarettes and Wrigley's Spearmint Gum. Kathy is not a morning person either, so we ride to school silently on the bus, gazing expressionlessly out the window bobbing and bouncing as the bus bumps and jiggles along old York Road.

Towson is a suburb just north of Baltimore City. It is an average east coast town, peppered with a mixture of brick row houses and two-story split levels made with half-brick and half-wood paneling. Just on the outer edge of Towson, there's Lutherville, Dulaney Valley and Ruxton, which consist of a mix of middle to upper middle-class and some very wealthy families.

The mustard colored, two-story, painted brick house that we reside in on Cavan Drive, falls into the working middle-class area just on the border of Towson and Lutherville. It is a nice safe neighborhood with the majority of households split between mostly Wasps and Catholics. It is common to see girls in plaid uniforms and boys in blue twill suits and khakis, also waiting on the corner for their bus to the local Catholic or prep school. Catholic Schools are big here and a popular option for those who don't want to send their kids to public schools. In the summer there is lots of lush and thick greenery everywhere with big old Oaks, Maples and Pine trees covering the landscape. The homes are a mix of seventies style split levels, and old New England and Victorian style two and three-story homes that have beautiful big wrap around front porches. For the most part, we live in a tidy neighborhood where the lawns and hedges are kept well trimmed and maintained. In the summer, the neighborhood comes to life with color as people plant colorful seasonal flowers around their walkways and yards. Summers are hot and very humid, but make for a beautiful and woodsy place to live. The nights are usually cool and lit up with lightning bugs, that we all loved to catch as little kids. Loch Raven Reservoir is only a few miles away and is a favorite place for the high school kids to spend the summer. It is a large lake and water reservoir, surrounded by thick, lush woods. All

the messenger

of us go there to swim, listen to music and have bonfire parties, and other teenage things.

Today, however, is just another gloomy winter Monday in Towson. The sky is grey; the trees and grass are brown and the cars are driving with their headlights on as the rain falls. The air is damp and cold and all I want to do is go home, put on my sweats and crawl back into my bed in the attic and be warm.

The bus turns off York Rd and into the parking lot of Towson High. It squeaks to a stop and drops us off at the front doors. In spite of the fact that I am not a morning person, the mornings are my favorite part of the day next to lunch. We have about 25 minutes to just hang out with our friends and talk about all the usual things that teenagers talk about – boys, music, parents and what we did over the weekend.

In the morning, the "freaks" all hang out behind the school or in the far corner of the parking lot so they can smoke. The freaks typically have long hair and are the residual generation that seems to still connect closely with the hippies of the seventies. They love black leather and blue jeans and prefer to listen to southern rock like Lynyrd Skynard and Neil Young or Pink Floyd, Zeppelin and more recently AC/DC and Black Sabbath. You can see them every morning leaning against their dark green Chevelle's, Fastback Mustang's and Black Trans Am's, with their arms either crossed, or thumbs tucked in their front pockets they are always projecting their general "badass-ness."

In high school, we are largely defined by the groups that we belong too, which are largely defined by the music we listen too and the clothes that we wear. It is sort of a tribal thing that allows us to identify quickly and easily which group we belong to and which people we associate with.

Then there are the "Preps." They tend to hang out in the cafeteria in the morning and are usually involved in all the school activities, such as student government, the school newspaper, math club, cheerleading and sports. If they are not in the cafeteria in the morning, you will find them in the gymnasium, sitting in the bleachers or playing hackee sack. The preps are full of energy and are always peppy and cheery about school. They are usually clothed in pale shades of green, pink and yellow sweaters, layered over polo style pique shirts, with alligators on the breast, and matching plaid pants or khakis. The jocks and cheerleaders usually belong to this group and they are typically good students.

When they *come* to school, the "head bangers," usually hang out right in front of the school by the front doors. They are not usually morning people either and typically don't say much. Their usual way of greeting each other in the morning is with a nod of the head and a "*t'sup?*" which translates to "what's up?" They are known for having big, long hair, which is spiky on top and for wearing lots of brightly colored animal prints, especially zebra. They are also fond of leather. However, in addition to black, their crowd is also known to wear red, yellow, blue or any other brightly colored leather. They typically adorn themselves with lots of leather belts and wristbands made of leather and steel spikes. Their music of choice is heavy metal like Metallica, Judas Priest, The Scorpians, Poison, Wasp and Van Halen. Their life and world revolves around listening to music and playing in bands. They are all aspiring musicians – a mix of drummers, singers and guitar players and a few of the guys wear eye liner.

The punk rockers congregate in a corner of the hall next to the cafeteria, lined up against a wall or sitting in a small circle on the floor. They are the artsy crowd and feature lots of multicolored hair, ranging from bright and opaque shades of red, blue, purple, to of course, jet black. They usually prefer to clip their hair into short, edgy geometric shapes with spikes and lots of very stiff hair gel. They typically like to shop at the local army supply store, Salvation Army or second-hand thrift stores where they find vintage clothes in varying shades of worn out and faded grey and black – lots of black. Converse high-tops in a variety of colors, along with black army boots, are a staple of their wardrobe and while you will also see them adorning their bodies with bands of spiked leather, they are more likely to wear them around their necks than waist. They also have lots of piercings in unusual places. The other groups look at them as the weird ones – the social misfits of the school. However, the members of this group do not mind that label at all. In fact, they actually revel in it and even strive for it. They are all about rebellion, anti-establishment and revolution. They are mostly just rebels without a cause, but their lives revolve around their artistic expression, being different and the freedom to be themselves. They strive to stand out, all the while projecting an attitude that they don't really care what anyone thinks. They have an experimental nature and are known to dabble in just about anything that may test cultural boundaries. The girls favor black lip stick and fingernails and the boys also have been known to wear eye liner. They are usually listening to The Ramones, The Cure, Psychedelic Furs, U2 or the latest new wave music like Devo or A Flock of Seagulls.

the messenger

As with all the generations, there are of course the nerds who tend to be inconspicuous and generally do not stand-out, preferring to just blend in. Of course, they are the good students and are probably in their classes studying before school, although I am not sure, as I do not report to my first class until the very last minute. I imagine they will end up being the ones in our class who will grow up to be the most successful, in spite of their low profile and unrecognized status in high school.

I step off the bus and make my way into the front of the school, past the head bangers and through the glass double front doors. I get down the hall to the cafeteria where the punkers are and I take a seat on the floor, next to Ellie. My black clothes and pink leather blend in well and in this group I am not particularly noticeable. We all have art class together and that is where we excel and prefer to be. School is dull and boring to us, except within art class where we are free to express ourselves and be different. Although I have friends from all the groups, it is here that I feel most comfortable, with the offbeat and artsy crowd and where I can just be myself.

Chapter 2
Passion and Discovery

Passion and Discovery

From my place on the floor, I can easily see through the windows and doors at the front of the school. I can see clearly, the head bangers hanging out under the roof that covers the front walkway. Ellie is babbling away in my ear about her weekend with Chris and Mike at the 8x10, an underage club downtown. There are several clubs in Baltimore that allow 18-year-olds to enter even though the drinking age is twenty-one. Once inside, different colored wrist bands clearly distinguish those who are eligible to drink from those who are not. They also do not tend to pay very close attention to the validity of the fake IDs that we all show up with, which are relatively easy to obtain from a variety of student sources. It is quite easy to get alcohol once in the door. Some of the underage clubs only serve soda, but of course, all the kids manage to sneak in miniature bottles of rum to spike the Cokes.

Ellie is a cute girl with brown hair and a bob cut that she likes to color with varying shades of mostly red and purple. She has a huge secret crush on Mike, who is not aware of it. However, she had resigned herself to be happy as a good buddy of his and Chris's. Mike is Chris' best friend and the three of them are like the Three Musketeers. Ellie was busy telling me how they had spent Saturday shopping at the downtown Salvation Army and Sonny's Surplus Army Supply Store, picking up various vintage clothing items and new black combat boots. She continues telling me that Saturday evening was spent at the Marble Bar, an underage club where they listened to Reptile House, a local house band which plays a mix of all the latest new wave music.

The Marble Bar is a really cool place located in the heart of downtown Baltimore. It is situated in between an old Byzantine looking Catholic cathedral and an abandoned textile factory. It is artsy and edgy and looks and feels like you are stepping back in time, into a piece of history. The outside entrance resembles the architecture and design of ancient Greece, complete with archways and columns which lead to huge arched wooden double doors. Once inside, the walls are marble and covered with cracks, water stains and all the evidence of the old building's age and state of disrepair. Beautiful old crystal chandeliers, with glass bulbs made to look like candelabras, hang from the ceilings and cast a dim golden glow over the marble walls. The floors are glossy and tiled, resembling the marble walls in color and texture. They are lined with electric wall sconces which resemble candles in candle holders. The candle wall sconces, which follow a line around the room, accent the beautiful arched windows that line the east and west sides of the building. They cause the inside of the building to resemble an old church. I heard that it used to be called the Crystal Ballroom and was used as an old ballroom for high society affairs. It must have been quite exquisite in its day, because even now, in its state of disrepair, to all of us, it's as if it is an ancient, gothic, place full of romance and magic where vampires would have hung out. For our crowd, it is the ultimate trendy and cool place to be. There is no furniture or chairs, just a big empty space with a small stage at the opposite end of the room. By midnight the room is wall to wall with spiked multi-colored haired kids, standing or dancing to the beat of new wave music.

While Ellie was busy chirping away about Saturday evening, I saw him through the glass double doors. My heart races and my palms began to sweat as I watch him stop in front of the doors to talk to the lead singer in his band David. Ellie's voice trails off into the distance as I focus my attention and eyes on him, Julian. He is tall and thin with a typical rock and roller build. He is dressed in a Van Halen t-shirt, blue jeans and red leather jacket. He is a head banger with long dark wavy brown hair, which is slightly spiky on top and drapes down over his shoulders, framing his exquisitely chiseled face and cheekbones. I am particularly attracted to the shape of his mouth – how it turns up just a little at the corners and smiles to reveal a beautiful set of teeth. I have always been attracted to nice teeth. His caramel brown eyes are deep set and intense. He transferred to our school about a month ago with his brother Nick, and I first noticed him in art class. Mr. Murphy the art teacher sat him in the empty seat right next

the messenger

to me. I am not usually into the head banger types, but Julian is different. There is something about him that is just...different.

Julian's brother, Nick, is a year younger than us and is a member of the preppy crowd. They ride the bus to school together, but once dropped off, go their separate ways. Nick walks past his brother, through the front doors, to the cafeteria. He is usually dressed in pastel polo shirts with alligators and matching plaid pants or blue jeans. Although Julian dresses more flamboyant and is artistic, he is more introverted and quiet. I have only noticed him speaking to small groups of friends. Otherwise, he mainly keeps to himself. I have a few classes with Julian and most of the time I observe him just doodling in his notebook – comic book characters mostly, and Batman. He seems to be a big fan of Batman.

Nick is just the opposite. From what I have observed – and I love to watch people – Nick is very outgoing, social, and in a very short time, has managed to make friends with just about everyone in Towson High. He is funny, sometimes loud and is always surrounded by a large entourage of friends. From what I can see, he is the life of the party. I have never actually spoken to Nick; in fact, I don't believe he is even aware that I exist. The preps do not typically pay any attention to the punkers; they think we are just weird. Nick is a good looking guy, tall like his brother but not as thin, and he is thicker and stockier in build. He has thick blonde hair and blue eyes and the same nice smile and teeth. Most people would not know they are brothers by the way they look with the exception that they are both strikingly good looking, have an extra dose of charisma – a unique and unusual energy about them that just causes both of them to stand out in a crowd.

"Denise, are you listening to a word I am saying?" asks Ellie

"Huh? Yea of course, sounds like you had a lot of fun." I said, knowing full well that indeed, I had not heard a word she had said.

"I just asked you a question. You are definitely not listening to me, you didn't hear a word I s..." Allie's eyes followed my eyes down the hall to where they rest on Julian. She turns back to look at me.

"Okay now I see why you are not listening, have you talked to him yet?" she asks.

"Uh...Nooo." I said sarcastically, eyes still fixed on Julian's perfectly sculpted face and long thick brown hair. He had a certain charisma that just stood out, making it impossible not to notice him.

"You have sat next to him everyday in art class for a month and you have not said anything to him?"

"Well, he hasn't said anything to me either; he doesn't even really look at me. Have you heard if he has a girlfriend? I never see him with anyone," I ask, with eyes still firmly fixed on Julian.

"I don't think so; I hear he keeps pretty much to himself except when he is playing in his band. I don't think he goes out much, he is never at any of the clubs or parties," she says as she shrugs her shoulders and looks back at him. "Hey, I did hear from Todd Baker that his band is playing at a cabin at the end of Black Rock Road for the bonfire party this weekend. We could go if you want." Ellie's eyes widen at the thought of embarking on a new adventure. We never go to the head banger parties, but Ellie is always up for an adventure.

"We could dress up as head bangers," she continues. "It will be fun and you will get to meet Julian! I think he just is not that into school. Maybe if you meet him out, you two will hit it off. I think he likes you, he's just shy." Ellie feels confident in this assessment based on her observation from her advantageous position on the opposite side of the rectangle in art class. Our desks are arranged into two rectangles

She tells me that she has seen him checking me out a few times and tells me again that she really thinks he likes me.

Julian walks by us, talking to David and for one brief moment looks in my direction, making eye contact. My heart stops and I freeze. But just like that, he looks away as he walks by and I watch him walk to the end of the hall and into Mr. Daniel's class.

"Okay, I'll go. Do you think your Mom will give you the car?"

Chapter 3
Surprises and Beautiful Music

Surprises and Beautiful Music

Finally it is Friday and I noted, while eating my Lucky Charms this morning that the weatherman said that Baltimore could expect some unseasonably warm weather for November this weekend. The forecaster said that Saturday and Sunday would be in the mid to upper fifties and we could expect warmer nights with temperatures hovering in the upper forties – just perfect for the bonfire party with Julian on Saturday night. Although I am excited about going to the party and at the prospect of having a chance to meet Julian out of school, the idea of standing around in a thin leather jacket while temps slip down into the frosty zones is not my idea of fun.

I can hardly wait for Saturday, I think to myself, while I gaze out the windows of the school bus. As we pass by a giant billboard featuring President Reagan with the slogan "Just Say No," I cannot help but wonder how that billboard could possibly have any affect on the people I knew experimenting with recreational drugs. *What a waste of billboard space*, I think to myself.

Todd, who is sitting in the seat in front of me, turns around to ask, "Hey Deese, do you want to go to the Marble Bar this weekend? Reptile House is playing on Saturday."

The Marble Bar was strictly an underage club, which served no alcohol or drinks and was officially BYOB, so getting into the club was never a problem for us.

"Oh, no I can't I'm going somewhere with Ellie on Saturday, but we could hit the matinee at the Charles Theatre on Sunday if you want. They are showing the *Rocky Horror Picture Show* again this weekend," I reply.

"OK, cool, that sounds good." Todd's house is less than a mile away from mine, but in a much nicer neighborhood. He lives in one of those big houses in Dulaney Valley. I always like going to his house and seeing his dad who is really funny and reminds me of Rodney Dangerfield.

The bus squeaks to a stop in front of the glass doors, and as we file off the bus I scan the head bangers group to see if Julian is in school today. I wouldn't say he missed a lot of school, but he missed more than most and he often had a habit of coming to school late. I figure he must not be much of a morning person either. When his mom doesn't drop his brother and him off, he arrives on the bus about ten minutes after my bus drops us off. Nope, he's not here yet. I say bye to Todd, who is off to talk to a group of seniors, and head through the glass doors to my group in the corner. I sit down next to Ellie, who is frantically doing some last minute cramming for her world history test first period.

"Hey do you think JJ would go to the bonfire with us tonight? I ask Ellie. "He seems to have become pretty friendly with Julian and he is just so funny maybe he could help break the ice a little. We should ask him at lunch, what do you think?"

JJ is about the funniest kid we know, he makes us laugh and is always acting silly. He does not really fit into any of the groups at school – he is his own group. He prefers to keep his afro shaved close to the head with a short Mohawk running down the middle. He sometimes dresses preppy and sometimes like Morris Day or MC Hammer. He is in our art class and keeps us laughing with his impressions of Morris Day singing Jungle Love. The most memorable thing about JJ is his gregarious laugh. His dark skin accentuates his perfect white teeth and great smile. He is full of life and provides most of the comic relief in class. This makes him very popular with the class but not very popular with Mr. Murphy, our art teacher.

I cannot help but notice that in the brief time that Julian has been in our art class he, JJ and Gary have really hit it off. They are always laughing and clowning and keeping Ellie and I entertained. Julian, who seems to be rather quiet and aloof in school, loosens up quite a bit in art class and can become even animated and funny, clowning around with Gary and JJ. I can see why he is in a band; he definitely has a performer side.

"Sounds good to me, I'm sure JJ will wanna go," Ellie acknowledges.

the messenger

"He likes that kind of music anyway and plus he is always fun to hang out with. I'll ask him," she says.

I take my seat in art class and heave my overstuffed back-pack on to the desk and start digging around for my sketchbook and pencils. Julian isn't here yet and Ellie is over on the other side of the room chatting with Mike and Chris. In usual fashion, JJ is in the hall laughing and clowning with Gary and I feel nervous and sick to my stomach trying to think of what I should say. Just then, I look up to see Julian walking through the door, right in front of our desks. He sits down next to me and proceeds to start rooting through his back-pack. No one else is at our rectangle and for some reason Mr. Murphy is late and not in the room yet. This is my perfect chance.

"I heard your band is playing at the bonfire party this weekend," I say. I hate my voice and the sound of the words as they come out of my mouth. All I ever wanted was one of those cute little high pitched girl voices, like the preppy girls have, but no. Instead, I have to have this raspy, deep gravely voice – the very voice that caused so much taunting and teasing in grade school and junior high. I hate the sound of my voice and immediately feel like I must have sounded stupid. I can't even look at him and instead look at the desk nervously.

It's funny, because I would not say that I am normally a shy girl, and in most situations, I socialize quite easily. I think of myself as pretty outgoing really and will usually talk to just about anyone for that matter. But, something about Julian makes me nervous, almost dizzy when he is around. He stops rummaging in his backpack and looks straight at me – right in my eyes and I freeze. He pauses for a moment just looking at me for a few seconds – which to me seems like an eternity – and then raises his eyebrows with an expression of surprise. He smiles slightly, just enough that his lips do that adorable little curling up at the ends. I am speechless and am assuming that he must be surprised that I have said anything to him.

"Yeah, we are....are you going?" his eyes are still on mine, dark and intense, making it hard for me to look at him, but totally impossible to look away.

"Well, a bunch of my friends are talking about going, so yeah, I was thinking of going too." I am trying very hard not to fidget and hope that I do not look as nervous as I feel. Julian on the other hand appears totally calm and at ease.

"Really?" he says with that same surprised look and raising of the eye brows. It's as if this time, he is saying he finds that hard to believe. "I didn't think you and your friends were into the kind of music we play."

I lie and say "Oh yeah, we are into all kinds of music, plus the bonfire parties are always a lot of fun." Well it wasn't a total lie; I did like a few metal bands like the Scorpions and Van Halen. Didn't that count as their kind of music?

"Well cool then, I guess I'll see you there." This time, his smile and expression seemed pleasantly surprised and maybe even a little excited. I couldn't be sure, but I thought in that moment that Ellie may just be right after all.

I have always had this uncanny knack for reading people. I can just tell how they feel, and sometimes what they are thinking and even things about them that I'm not sure they themselves even know. I couldn't tell you how I know these things, I just know and I never doubt or question what I know about people. I am pretty much a human lie detector and can spot a fraud or some one lying right away. This innate ability causes my mother much stress I think, as she can never figure out just how I know such things or how I could say such things about people. I think in her mind, I have been a very precocious child. But I know what I know, and can see what I can see about people and that is just the way it is. I don't spend much time thinking about how or why I know, I just do. The only problem with this ability I have is that it does not work at all with guys, at least not the ones I am interested in. It seems the minute my emotions get involved, I lose the ability to read that person. So Julian is a mystery to me – a complete and total mystery. I have no idea what he is thinking or feeling and can't read him very well at all. I suspect this is why he makes me so nervous. I have never felt this way about someone before and quite frankly, it is making me feel a little crazy.

Having these abilities, or gifts as some people would say, has been both a blessing and a curse at the same time, and kind of a double edge sword. On one hand I have always felt that they give me an unfair advantage in life, allowing me to easily see what is as invisible as the wind to others. However, at the same time, I also have the painful ability to feel others feelings and pick up their thoughts, often when they are about me. High school can be rough and kids can be cruel, and being a teenager is awkward enough without having to know and feel what everyone else is thinking about you all the time. There are times when I wish I didn't have

the messenger

this ability and that I would just be normal. But I'm not, so instead, I work hard at pretending to be normal and keep most of what I know to myself. I have learned that that is the best thing to do; no one knows about my abilities, not my mom, not Ellie not anyone.

My knowing things have made stuff kind of difficult between me and my mom, as much for her as for me I imagine. It's complicated with her and me. To the best of my understanding, I have decided that this uncanny ability I have of just "knowing things" makes my mom incredibly uncomfortable. She refuses to acknowledge it or even talk about it, but at the same time, seems very unnerved by it. She prefers living her life seeing only what she wants to see and I simply don't have that luxury. I see things as they are, whether I want too or not and whether I like what I see or not. To add insult to injury, since my mom and Francis had my baby brother and sister, my mom has decided the whole family should start going to church. Now don't get me wrong, I have nothing against church or my mother's efforts to create a better family atmosphere, it's just the *types* of churches that my mom seems to be drawn too that I have a problem with. For some reason they all tend to be the fire and brimstone types, that are continually warning that the end times are near. And, they seem to be focused more on all the things we shouldn't do rather than all the joy and beauty life has to offer. They are also not particularly approving or accepting of people like me – people who are different and have these unusual abilities. We have tried several churches over the years, but to me they all seem basically the same in that they liken people like me to witches and witchcraft, which is still difficult for me to understand in the twentieth century. The bottom line is that I just don't feel comfortable in any of them. Thankfully she does not make me go anymore, and I am grateful to her for that.

Mr. Murphy walks in, slightly out of breath and in a rush, as if he had just run up the two flights of stairs that lead to the art room. He calls the class to attention. As we normally do, we all begin to work on our projects while chatting away about what we are going to do this weekend. Julian and I do not say anything else to one another until the bell rings. Then, he turns to look at me and with that same sweet smile and flashing me those beautiful and intense caramel brown eyes, he flings his back pack up on to his shoulder and says "I guess I'll see you tomorrow." My heart stops.

I have always been fascinated by musicians. Being an artist myself, I have a great appreciation for their artistic nature and expression. I have respect for the way they can put themselves so out there, in front of a crowd just doing their thing – what ever their thing may be. I don't think that I could ever get up in front of a crowd like that. Part of the reason that I believe I have always been fascinated by musicians is because I do not have one smidgen of musical ability myself. I tried learning the violin once but dropped it pretty quickly, when I realized I really just didn't have much of a talent for music. I have always been amazed at how people can create and make music and even more amazed by their ability to hear sounds and then recreate them. This is as foreign to me as speaking in another language.

Chapter 4
The Beginning of the End

The Beginning of the End

The bonfire party was fun and Julian hung out with us in between his sets. We had plenty of time to talk and get to know each other a little more. He invited me to ride home from the party along with him and the band in their van. The ride home was filled with laughter and chatter as the six of us, Julian's band and me, headed back to Towson in the silver van. Julian and I sat in the very back next to each other, leaning up against the double doors. The rest of the passengers paid no attention to us as they laughed and joked and discussed the set they just played and all the technical aspects of the acoustics and sound. Julian was pressed up tight against me, the zebra striped guitar resting between his legs, as we squeezed in between the two large amplifiers. We talked about school, our families, and music. It seemed like not a second passed that was not filled with our conversation; we had so much to say to one another. I realized in that moment, that it was as if I had known him forever; there was a connection between us that just defied logic. I felt so comfortable with him, like I was reuniting with a really close old friend – someone I had known forever and I wondered if he felt it too? For a moment, in the back of that van, we were all alone – completely alone in our own universe and time stopped.

From that night forward, Julian and I were inseparable. We spent the next two years doing all the usual high school stuff – hanging out with our friends, going to the movies, to see bands play and of course to the senior prom. I went to all their shows to support my guitar player boyfriend and when were not out with the band we were usually at Julian's house watching movies, hanging out and listening to music. Julian lived in a small apartment, not far from school, with his mom and brother. My senior year when Mom and Francis sold the house on Cavan Drive to get a bigger house in the country, I began staying some nights with my grandparents. They lived close to my school allowing me to avoid the nearly one hour drive out to the country. After graduation, I enrolled at Towson University, which was right across from the high school. I also began spending more and more time at Julian's which was also close by.

I preferred spending time at Julian's where I felt most comfortable rather than be at home. I would say that I have always felt different – like I didn't fit in and, and now that my Mom had remarried and started a new family, I felt more like an outsider than ever. I really did not fit in with her new life and being at home just made me feel like I was a burden and in the way. I, as any college student would be, wanted to be out with friends, discovering life and seeing the world. Julian's mom practically adopted me, as I was at her home more often than not during my first two years of college. She also did not seem to mind if I stayed at their house from time to time to avoid making the drive back home late at night. I also grew very fond of Nick over the years, whom I came to think of as my own brother.

Nick remained the life of the party and was quite the party-goer in those days. He lived life a bit on the wild side and with reckless abandon; Julian and I were not big party-goers and were usually home when Nick would come in during the early morning hours. He always came bursting in like a tornado laughing, joking and entertaining us with stories of the evening's escapades. We looked forward to his arrival.

By the end of my second year of college, as with many high school sweethearts, Julian and I realized we were growing in different directions and split to pursue separate paths. I was finishing up my second year of college and beginning to seriously focus on my goals and career ambitions. Julian was pursing his dream of being a musician and was growing increasingly frustrated with the limited opportunities in Baltimore. He decided that the only way to make it big and find real opportunity would be to move to LA.

As much as I wanted to go with him – to follow him - I knew I could not live the life of a musician's girl and, I knew I had my own things to do even though I was not entirely sure yet what they were. I also knew that one day, I wanted to have a family and settle down and I did not want to do that with a husband who was always on the road. Plus, Julian had his sights set on much bigger things than settling down with a girl in Baltimore and he needed the freedom to pursue his dreams. No, the futures that we imagined for ourselves just did not fit together anymore and no amount of passion could change that.

To this day, I remember vividly, a spring night a few weeks before he was to go. We were outside and the sky was unusually clear. I could see all the stars and the magnificent full moon. The air was cool and dry with the lingering smell of winter which was beginning to mingle with the freshness of green grass and the first blossoms of spring. I was struggling with how to come to terms with the decision that we had made because I was still so desperately in love with him. As we stood under the stars facing one another, he wrapped his arms around me, kissed my forward and looked into my eyes... with that look, the same look that could instantly bring me to my knees. "You know I will always love you," he said.

I did know and I said to him, "One day we are going to find each other again, and I'll probably be married with kids, but I know somehow, someway, we will." And once again, my heart stopped, but this time for a different reason than it had when we first met. This time, my heart stopped because it was suddenly and violently ripped in half.

And, as a testament to my uncanny gift of being able to just "know things," without my even realizing it at the time, I would come to learn that I would not understand how true that statement really was... for another 20 years.

A few weeks later, we said our goodbyes and went our separate ways. I drove Julian to the airport. He had only a small bag and his guitar case in hand. I watched him get on the plane to Los Angeles and I cried. I cried all the way home and I cried for weeks to follow. For the many years that followed I often wondered how he was and how his life had turned out. It's something I imagine all high school sweethearts must do.

From time to time, I did hear bits and pieces about Julian and Nick over the years, but once I moved to Key West I heard very little. The last thing I ever heard came about ten years after I moved to Key West. I learned that Julian had moved to Las Vegas with his band and then back to LA where he worked as a comic book artist. The news made me happy for him because I had always believed he was an amazingly talented artist – much more so than me. It was good to see that all those doodles of Batman that he had drawn in high school had actually paid off, turning into a successful career for him.

For a few years after college, I stayed in Baltimore living in an apartment with two roommates while bartending a few nights a week at a bar by the water downtown. My senior year, I received an internship as a graphic designer at an Ad agency, which after graduation became a full-time position. As time went on, however, I grew increasingly dissatisfied with my career choice and equally so with the long, dreary, winters in Baltimore. I began to contemplate my options for something more.

A little disillusioned with my initial launch into adult life, and young and anxious for a change of scenery, some fun in the sun, and a new purpose in life, I emptied my apartment, sold most of my worldly things, packed my car and bags and headed to Key West. Like so many others before me, I went in search of my purpose. It took awhile – about 12 years actually – but eventually, I found it.

Chapter 5
"Love My Way and It's a New Day"

– The Psychedelic Furs

"Love My Way and It's a New Day"
– The Psychedelic Furs

I open my eyes to look out the glass French doors, which are open and lead onto the second story balcony of the bedroom of our two story conch home. I roll over to look at the alarm clock, which is playing my favorite eighties play list on the iPod. It's 8:05 and The Psychedelic Furs are singing "Love My Way". I still love eighties music, it just makes me feel happy. Plus, if I must wake to the alarm, I prefer to hear my vintage music, to a buzzer or the voice of the local radio rock jock. The fact is that I really prefer to just wake up when I wake up - when my body is ready to wake up. I will never like being awakened by an alarm in the middle of a good dream, as I tend to sleep very deeply and dream almost nightly.

I have very vivid dreams and have no trouble remembering them. In fact, for as long as I can remember and since I was a very young girl, I can recall dreams I have had of future events before they even happen. I have many times dreamed about natural disasters, like the tsunami that hit Southeast Asia a few years back. I dreamed about it just about two weeks before it happened. I didn't know where or when it was going to happen, but I knew it was coming. I have often wondered why I dream about random events that I have no control over and no way of stopping. I have come to the conclusion that I am just sort of like a finely tuned radio receiver, which at night just randomly scans and inadvertently picks up different frequencies. Thus, I just tune in and pick up all sorts of random information while sleeping, that is essentially quite useless, but invariably, turns out to be repeatedly accurate and true.

I have dreamed of countless future events such as; earth quakes, train wrecks, floods and plane crashes over the years. Many of my business ideas have come to me in dreams where I often receive important messages. I have also on a few occasions been known to tap into the dreams of my significant others while we are sleeping next to one another.

In one particular case I had gone away for the weekend with a man I was dating before I married my husband. I woke up in the morning to tell him that I had a very strange and vivid dream about his family in New York. He was an italian man; raised Catholic and who I eventually figured out was in the mob. I had never told him about my abilities. In fact, I usually made a point of not telling men I dated about them. I had learned that if they did not think I was crazy, they would invariably be uncomfortable knowing that I might be able to read their thoughts or see things they might not want me to see. Not knowing at the time that I had been dreaming his dream, I went on to describe in detail my dream, which took place at his aunt's house in New York. Several of his relatives were there to attend a cousin's wedding, that we were also there to attend. He was completely freaked out when I told him about my dream and he sat straight up in bed with a confused look on his face and exclaimed "Oh my God, that was my dream! How could you know that?" With a puzzled look on his face, he thought for a moment and then asked, "Whose dream was that, mine or yours?" I said, "Well obviously it was your dream, as I have never been to your aunt's house or met any of your relatives."

Poor guy, he was understandably unnerved as I imagine most men would be if they knew that their wife or girlfriend could see their dreams! So, I have learned to pay very close attention to my dreams, which is why I do not like interrupting my sleep, or my dreams, with the alarm.

To me sleeping is like creative down time and is as important to my work and my life as anything that I do while I'm awake. For instance, the main reason that I live in Key West is because of a dream. For much of my adolescence and early adult life, I had reoccurring dreams about swimming in the ocean and being able to breathe underwater. I must have had the same dream at least twenty times in my life, which led me into an obsession to learn to scuba dive. Yes, I moved to Florida to learn how to scuba dive.

I moved just after college, only intending to stay for a year to have some fun. Then my plan was to move back to Baltimore, get a job and join the real world. However, like so many others who live in Key West, that was 15 years ago and I'm still here.

the messenger

I lay my head back down on the pillow, and try to wake up. I gaze once again through the French doors at the clear blue sky and palm leaves, swaying gently in the island breezes just beyond my balcony. The balcony which is covered with pink bougainvillea overlooks a quaint tropical garden and pool that are both typically small and characteristic of most Key West homes. The garden is surrounded by a ten foot wooden privacy fence, which is flanked by a lush blanket of palms, pink, red and orange bougainvillea and yellow and red hibiscus. All the conch houses on Elizabeth Street are surrounded by privacy fences. This is due to the fact that the entire island is only 4 x 6 miles and the houses are squished into every little nook and cranny of space available on the very small island. That, coupled with the fact that Key West is inhabited by roughly twenty-five thousand year-round residents (and double that in the winter months), makes having space and privacy a very valuable and sought after commodity on the island. Living in Key West, with such a shortage of land and space, we find space on the very beautiful and vast crystal clear turquoise tropical waters that surround the island, where the Gulf meets the Atlantic.

Practically everyone in Key West either owns a boat or works on one, and if you are one of the few who doesn't, you know someone who does. So the matrix of life in Key West revolves around the sun and the water. It is why we all pack onto this small little island, pay exorbitant rents and tolerate never ending droves of pleasure seeking tourists who come looking for cheeseburgers in Paradise, Jimmy Buffet, margaritas in Margaritaville, and the chance to catch the ever elusive Blue Marlin like Ernest Hemingway. Of course, I can't forget to mention the seductive and intoxicating lure of Duval Street and Fantasy Fest, which comprise the ultimate smorgasbord of anything goes uninhibited adult fun in paradise.

It is another beautiful and balmy day in Key West as tropical breezes and sunshine make their way through the doors of the balcony and gently cascade in ripples across my face and bed. It is almost enough to inspire me to be a morning person. I take a moment to just lay there and bask in the beauty of this island paradise and consider how fortunate I am to be spending my winters here and not in Baltimore. Luckily, there is never a shortage of sunshine and warm weather in Key West.

Sage, my dog, is stretched out at the foot of the bed, his head resting on my foot. He hasn't a care in the world. I rescued him from a local animal rescue, that in turn had rescued him from the Miami pound just before they were about to put him down. He was 6 weeks old. Our best guess is that he is a husky-shepherd mix with a black coat of fluffy soft husky fur that is marked by patches of white and tan on his face and underbelly. He has a fluffy curled husky tail and one blue eye and one brown eye. Where ever we go, people always stop to comment on his beautiful eyes.

Sage goes just about everywhere with me and prefers to go without a leash, which is not a problem with most places in Key West. The myriad of outdoor restaurants and tiki bars, are quite hospitable to well behaved dogs. It's funny, I find the dogs in Key West are just as laid back as the people, and I attribute that to the intense heat and humidity. It is just too hot for them to fight or run around. They also don't seem to waste any time or energy chasing the enormous amount of stray cats that inhabit the small island. Most of the cats prefer to live around the restaurants where there is an unending supply of doting tourists to feed them scraps. At night, they hang around by the back doors of the restaurants where the workers feed them leftovers.

Just like the people in Key West, the dogs and cats live in complete peace and harmony, oblivious to their differences and the fact that they are supposed to hate each other.

It is nine and the bright room, filled with sunshine, makes getting out of bed much easier to tolerate. I make my way downstairs to put on a pot of Cuban espresso coffee. To the locals, it is pretty much known as liquid speed and is definitely not for beginners! Café con Leche is what I like to drink, which is basically a shot of Cuban espresso coffee and a heaping glass of steamed milk.

The old Cuban men, fourth and fifth generation conchs, can be found standing by Sandy's Café in the mornings, drinking shot glasses of the stuff and eating Cuban toast, while talking about the old days. Cuban toast is a great staple of the Key West diet. It is a white bread made with lard, that is sliced and sandwiched with butter and cheese inside, then flattened and pressed into a toasting machine. It is about the most fattening thing you can eat for breakfast, but it is so good. The combination of Cuban espresso and toast will cure even the worst Duval Street hangover. Yup, this stuff will get you going in the morning – even the worst morning person like me

My Blackberry is blinking on the kitchen counter, so I turn the ringer back on and begin to check my messages. The first one is from Javier, my husband, saying good morning. Javier, unlike me, is a morning person. He wakes up at the crack of dawn without an alarm clock, regardless of

the messenger

what time he goes to bed. He is also one of those people that doesn't need coffee in the morning, because he wakes up, jumps out of bed wide awake and refreshed. I cannot even comprehend this.

Javier is a very good looking man with long thick brown hair that he wears in a pony-tail at his neck. He has a very European looking face with high cheek bones, a strong square jaw and soft brown eyes. He has a thick Argentine-Spanish accent which most Americans mistake for French.

Javier has worked at several jobs since he moved to Key West from Argentina ten years ago. When I met him, he owned a martial arts school and was teaching Karate and Jui Jitsu to the local adults and kids alike.

His partner was also a very good-looking man with long dark hair, who was also from Argentina. Between the two of them, they managed to attract a never ending parade of female students for their very popular Kickboxing classes. Currently though, Javier captains a Catamaran which takes tourists on snorkeling tours to the reef and on Sunset cruises. He loves his job, gives a great tour and the people always love him.

I met Javier at his Karate School about a year and a half after my divorce. Chris my son, who was about five at the time, was having a difficult time with the divorce and I felt he might benefit from taking some Karate lessons. I too had always been interested in trying it myself, so together we signed up and well, the rest is history as they say.

Chris is fourteen now. He is a great kid that constantly reminds me of myself when I was his age. I get quite a kick out of the fact that he listens too much of the same music that I do now and did when I was his age. Chris would probably fall into the surfer skater crowd. He prefers to keep his sun bleached blond hair on the long side and is usually dressed in a trendy t-shirt and plaid shorts all donned with the latest hip surfer company logos. He is very proud about being born in Key West and having the proud privilege of being an official "Conch". He also loves the water and the beach and prefers to be fishing with his dad above all else. Between the two of them, they hold quite a few IGFA world records. Chris is with his dad today making preparations for the Sailfish Tournament this weekend, so the house is quiet.

The next message on my phone is from Bob Riley and he wants to talk to me about tonight's group. I have done a variety of work since graduating from Towson University and moving to Key West. My degree was in art, graphic design and marketing and I worked in that field for two years in Baltimore after graduation but I just found sitting behind a desk all day in an office to be tedious and unfulfilling. So, upon moving to Key West, I tried a bunch of odd jobs at first, focused more on having fun than on my career. I was twenty-four, single, and living in paradise. Who cared about work? I worked as a bartender, waitress, scuba diving instructor, St Pauli Girl beer model, personal trainer and professional make-up artist, to name just a few. I had a blast and there was no shortage of parties to attend and people to meet. Life was a party and I didn't want to miss anything.

    I am grateful that I never had a penchant for drugs, or even alcohol in excess; I mostly just enjoyed meeting different kinds of people and the adventure of it all. Key West is not the place to be for anyone struggling with those issues, that's for sure. For them, Key West would surely be like being a kid in a candy store. For me however, I was just enthralled with the architecture, the landscape and the very diverse, quirky and eclectic collection of people that called Key West home. It was all just so different than Baltimore and I was busy taking it all in and seeing the sights. I like to describe Key West as a small town where everyone knows everyone, but which has the diversity of people and cultures of a big city. It's what gives Key West its charm.

    However, too much of even a good thing can get boring eventually, and It didn't take too long for me to grow tired of the never ending parade of party's and party goers. So at twenty-seven, I started my first business and opened Key West's first and only tanning salon. Yes, I know, it sounds crazy, and that's what most people thought at the time. But, I laughed my way all the way to the bank as that little tanning salon on Duval Street turned out to be quite a little cash cow.

    Living and working in Key West is expensive, very expensive, and most people work two and some times even three jobs, just to pay the outrageous rents on the island. We are also people who live our lives in bathing suits, shorts and tank tops most of the time and everyone just looks better with a tan in summer clothes. So, with no time to go to the beach, and a chance to tan in just ten minutes in air-conditioned comfort, the locals were lined up at the door of my little salon. I even eventually expanded and opened a second location on the other side of the island, adding a full service Day Spa. It was also Key West's first full service Day Spa and it featured a prominent Miami Beach dermatologist who offered the latest advances in cosmetic dermatology, along with the usual services of massage, nails, tanning and the like. So, for the next twelve years, I spent my life ambitiously running a very successful and busy business. I

the messenger

sold the businesses not long after 9-11 and have been doing what I like to call "consulting" ever since.

I pick up the Blackberry and dial Bob Riley, "Hi Bob, its Denise, what do we have going for tonight?"

Chapter 6
A New Beginning

A New Beginning

"Hey Denise. Good to hear from you girl!" Bob's voice was always as enthusiastic and full of life as he was. "I just wanted to touch base with you for a minute before our group tonight. Without telling you too much, I just wanted to give you a heads up and let you know it looks like we are going to have a mixed bag tonight and six confirmed with a possible seventh."

"Okay, that sounds great. I'll see you at five then." I reply.

Bob and I have been working directly and indirectly together now for close to five years. He is a large man at about six feet, four inches, and has the build of a linebacker. He might be a scary man to have a confrontation with, were it not for the fact that he is such a gentle giant. Bob is in his mid sixties and is a former military man and war veteran. He has had a long, diverse and successful work history over the years as an entrepreneur and has dabbled in all sorts of businesses from auto sales to child care. During this time and for the past twenty years, he has very faithfully and consistently volunteered monthly to counsel those who have lost loved one's to suicide. He is incredibly good at what he does. With his gentle strength, stability and compassion, he has a wonderful way of making everyone in his support group feel safe, understood and at ease. He is truly an advocate for the vulnerable ones in the world and I have a great and endearing respect for him and the work that he does so selflessly for others.

Bob and I met through a twenty-year-old , non-profit organization called

Prospect Hope. This "Victim's Advocacy" agency received referrals directly from the medical examiner's office and local law enforcement agencies in the area. Prospect Hope, or PH, provided free support services and counseling for individuals and families who had lost loved ones through sudden, unnatural or accidental death circumstances. Those we helped had lost loved ones through tragedies such as; homicide, domestic violence, suicide, drug overdoses, car accidents and many other accidents.

  I worked there once a month, for two years volunteering my time doing readings for the different support groups. The readings I gave provided the families left behind, a last word with the loved one they lost. This same information would also provide the families with many times, unknown information, validation, much needed closure and peace. I was told by the counselors that my work with the groups, in many cases, greatly accelerated the healing and grieving process. Whenever I read for a grief or addiction support group, I ask that the group facilitator always be present so that they can assist with processing the information that comes through and integrate it into the work they are doing with the group.

  Bob headed the grief support group for those who had lost someone to suicide while, another counselor, Jane, worked with those who had lost loved ones by homicide and accidental means. She facilitated the groups we did together and was always present in every group I worked with. Jane was also the Victim's Advocate for the state attorney's office. PH had a strict confidentiality policy so I was never, before or after, told the names of the people I worked with, nor anything about the circumstances that led them to be there.

  My work at PH initially started when I was asked to read for one of the groups after a member, a mother who had lost her daughter, came to see my privately. She reported to the group about our reading and the details that I brought through concerning her daughter's death. Jane, who was initially very skeptical, reluctantly agreed to the group's request to have me come read for them. Against her better judgment, she called me to ask if I would be interested in coming to read for the group. It was obvious to me in the beginning that Jane was there to protect her clients. She was actually anticipating their disappointment after being "taken for a ride." And, although she was very skeptical of me and my ability at first, that changed quickly. After witnessing my work first hand, by the end of our first group together, she became a believer. Jane and I continued to work together with the different groups monthly, for the next two years.

the messenger

As word traveled about the successes in our sessions, the group began to integrate people from all of the different types of support groups hosted by the center. One week I might work with the folks who had lost some one by homicide, the next week, suicide and the next, car accidents and so on. Some weeks would be a mix of all of these groups in one.

I knew it was very important for all of those in attendance to know that Jane had not told me anything about their loved one's passing. That way, they would be able to believe the experience and the messages they received. When I was first called, the members wanted to know what I would charge. When I found out about the nature of the groups and that the organization was a non-profit, it was important to me to do the work on a volunteer basis and I told them it would be free.

Because I knew we were about to embark into unprecedented and groundbreaking territory, I also knew there would be critics and skeptics who would try to discredit me and my work. I anticipated that they would say that I was "victimizing victims" for personal gain. If I volunteered my time, no one could say that. Plus, because I had never done this type of work before, I was not sure how it was going to go. Finally, by volunteering my time, I knew it would allow many people, who might not have been able to afford my services but desperately needed them, to have a rare opportunity to have a last word or conversation with their loved one.

The group and I were fortunate in that, although many people might have questioned my legitimacy and credibility, NO ONE could or would ever question Jane's. She had been in her career for twenty years, working not only with the state's attorney's office and PH, but also with Mother's Against Drunk Drivers. Her professional credibility was impeccable and she was well respected for her honesty and integrity. Jane lent to me and my work as a medium her good name, and for that, I am forever grateful.

Jane retired at the end of the two years that we worked together and as she did, my work with Prospect Hope came to an end. At the same time Jane retired, a minister took over as President of the Board of Directors at Prospect Hope and I was, not surprisingly, told that my services were no longer needed. Interestingly, however, not long after I was let go, the married minister was relived of his position on the board when it was discovered that he was having an extra-marital affair with the center's manager and that she had become pregnant with their child. Also, several thousand dollars had gone missing. As has so often been my experience, people who have a lot to hide, usually do not like having me around.

With the new leadership on the Board, not long after Jane and I left the center, many of the staff followed suit, including Bob Riley. Committed to his work and his dedication for helping others, he went on to co-found his own Grief Support group and I joined with him there. I have now done this work over five years and to this day, he and I continue to help those who are in great pain and distress, to try and find both comfort and peace in the midst of their great loss. This work has been the most rewarding work that I have ever done. I will always be grateful to Jane and Bob for believing in me and giving me the opportunity to help so many people. Without their ability to see the value of my work and readings to help others, and their willingness to put their own reputations and good names on the line for me, none of this unprecedented work would have been possible.

I do not remember most of the readings that I do and within a matter of days, hours and sometimes even minutes, I will forget most of the words that have come out of my mouth during a reading. It is important to understand that, first of all, due to the sheer volume of people and spirits that I meet and speak with weekly, and because of the many years I have been doing this, it is not possible for my brain to remember that mountain of information. It is also important for me personally, to let go of the thoughts, feelings and memories that I relive during a reading because they are not mine – they do not belong to me. If I were to walk around with the memory of all the pain, suffering and tragedy that I relive with others every day, I would not be able to function. People often ask me if my gift is a burden, or how I do work with group after group of mothers who have lost children. And I can honestly say that no, it is not a burden. It is a blessing and an honor. It brings great comfort to those who desperately need it and the healing is not only for those still here, but also, for those who have passed on to the spirit side of life. My work has one purpose and one purpose only, and that is to help people by facilitating their healing. I am always as uplifted and enlightened by the messages that spirits bring through as their loved ones are. However, with all that being said, there are of course some people, spirits and readings that really stand out in my memory. They are the ones that have left such an impression, that I could never forget them.

One such reading is one of the early readings that I did with a group at Prospect Hope. As I remember, it was a full group of about eight that night.

It's summer and the tropical air is thick and damp, as it usually is in Key West during the summer months. The sun is low in the sky as I drive

the messenger

north on U.S. Highway1 on my way to Marathon Key where the center is located. PH is located in a two-story, gold colored, office building next to the Sheriff's department.

   I can see the small private planes flying over the water as they are taking off and landing in the distance at a small private airport located just across the street from the Sheriff's office. The sky to the west is colored with beautiful shades of pink, orange and gold as the sun begins its daily descent into the crystalline turquoise waters where the Gulf of Mexico meets the Atlantic Ocean. As I drive over the small bridge to Sugarloaf Key and look to the east, towards the Atlantic, I can see the beautiful vast ocean, giving no distinction as to where the sky ends and the water begins. The small mangrove islands that pepper the flats bordering the keys, seem to float among the fluffy white clouds reflecting from the sky above. Just under the bridge and beyond, but close to the shoreline, I can see the old spongers standing in their small and primitive flat hulled wooden skiffs. They hold long poles in their hands as they maneuver their way through the shallow waters, picking up sea sponges. On the north side of the bridge and on the east side of US 1, are stacks upon stacks, of literally hundreds of lobster and crab traps. They line the side of the road, as I approach Cud Jo Key and E Fish, the local seafood and fish market.

   By the time I reach the center, it's dusk, the sun has disappeared and the stars are beginning to illuminate the clear night sky. I love the keys at night; there is no sight more beautiful than the sky over the ocean on a clear night. With only a little land and mostly water, there is also little artificial light to be found. So when darkness falls, it seems as if you are floating inside a giant globe shaped planetarium. The stars reflect onto the dark blue water and the horizon becomes invisible. It is a magnificent sight to behold. If one is fortunate enough to be out in a boat on one of these breathtaking nights, and if the tide flows just right, you may be lucky enough to float into the midst of a colony of bioluminescence. They light up the sea around you with twinkling lights, much like a school of underwater fire flies. This underwater fireworks display only occurs in the summer when the water is very warm. It is quite a treasure to behold and a delight to scuba divers brave enough to go into the sea at night. It is also one of the main reasons I moved to Key West.

   I park the car in back of the building and proceed up the elevator to the second floor. No one else is here yet, except for Jane, who is finishing some work from her day in her office. I say "Hi" to let her know that I am here and proceed down the hall to the group's meeting room. I always do a short meditation prior to reading for a group to calm my mind, prepare myself and to check in with my helpers on the spirit side to see what I can expect for the readings. It is during this time that my spirit helpers will alert me to any difficulties or challenges that I may encounter during the group. It is also at this time, that I will many times meet in advance, the spirits that I will be speaking with throughout the evening. I have learned to keep these groups to about six or eight so that I have more time with each person. The needs and intensity of the circumstances and feelings involved in working with these types of groups requires a little more time than a normal group reading.

The group's room is understated and is scantily furnished with a worn couch and matching recliner on one side and office chairs on the other. There is a glass and wicker coffee table in the center and matching end table between the recliner and the couch. I arrange the chairs in a half circle in front of me, and place my chair at the center so that I can easily see everyone's faces. As are most office buildings, it's lit by fluorescent overhead lighting, which I don't like working under as I find fluorescent lighting to be harsh and it distorts the energy in the room. At my request, Jane turns off the overhead fluorescent lights and instead I turn on a table lamp in the corner and light a few candles.

Spirit has warned me that I have a pretty tough customer coming – a real skeptic, and that he is one of the two men attending and will sit to my right. I open the door sit down and wait for our guests to arrive. Jane shuffles a pile of papers from the day on her desk and then puts them away, closes the door to her office and joins me in the group's meeting room. We sit and chat for a moment as our guests begin to arrive and pick their seats. I have not met any of them before and Jane has not met some of them either because they have come from other groups hosted by the center. Jane always makes a point to speak with the counselor that works with each person prior to the group, to find out the details of the circumstances that brought the individual to the group. She does this to make sure that she is able to deal with any reactions and responses that may arise during the group and to follow up with everyone afterwards if needed.

There are many times in these groups that I have brought through information that is not known at the time by the person I am reading for, that will instead come to light in the future. For example, perhaps I may see prescription drugs being abused and in high doses in the body the night of a sudden death or suicide. With no evidence to support that, the night of the incident, a family may not know and be able to validate my information until they receive the medical examiner's report several months later. Jane will then be able to clarify and address this with that client at a later date. That one, very important detail, will then provide specific proof that I was really talking to someone's loved one when it is later verified to be true. By doing so, this also allows the person I gave the reading for to believe and accept any other messages the spirit felt was important to bring through to them during their reading. The proof is in the details and I always strive to bring through very personal and specific details about someone's life or death. I want to tell them things which I have no way of knowing or guessing, the more personal and detailed the better. Details that only the person I am reading for and the loved one passed over would know. This next story is a beautiful example of one such instance. It happened with the help of one very special spirit who was determined to get through to his loved one's.

I always take the first few moments to observe people as they enter the room and I will know almost immediately who is nervous, open and receptive, who is still deeply grieving and most definitely, who is a skeptic or a non-believer. I can feel people's energy or resistance as I scan them and the room. The skeptics will feel to me as if I am running into a brick wall like a big thud in the middle of the room. It is important to note that these are not groups of metaphysically minded seekers that would typically visit a psychic or medium. Most of the people in these groups have never and would never, visit a psychic or medium. Many come from very traditional religious backgrounds, beliefs and conditioning. Some are even atheists and do not believe in God or, for that matter, life after death. The only reason that they have come to see me is because someone has told them that I can speak to their loved one who is now passed. Desperate for peace, hope and relief from great pain and sometimes guilt, they come to me for answers and hoping for proof that their loved ones are ok. I have become very accustomed to working with people who have spiritual and intellectual barriers to accepting what I do. Some are still in denial and struggling with their grief and a few may even show up with hostility and disdain for what I do. Anyone who works with people in grief knows that everyone handles it differently, some of us better than others, and I have learned to be prepared to expect just about anything. Having Jane by my side has taught me much about the process of grief and how not to take the reactions personally. Therefore, I have developed a pretty thick skin which has helped me to remain confident, capable and committed in what I do.

As I intuitively begin to scan the room and the people in it, I introduce myself, my work and explain a little about how I work. I talk briefly about what the participants can expect and I give some quick instruction that serves to make my job a little easier. If needed, I spend a few minutes on a little small talk and some humor to help lighten the mood, make people feel more comfortable and relax. Throughout the evening, I will be constantly "psychically" scanning the people in attendance, while at the same time connecting with their loved ones in spirit. I am always aware and keeping close tabs on how each person is receiving the messages I am delivering and processing the whole experience. I can for the most part, tell if someone is open and accepting to what I am saying, or closed, fearful or resistant. This work takes the term multitasking to a whole other level. It's a good thing I am pretty good at multitasking.

It is quite common in these groups, because we are dealing with people who may have passed by suicide or may have had mental health issues and addictions, that the family members will still be in denial about their loved one's problems before their death. The denial aspect alone can cause quite a bit of resistance and friction between me and the person that I'm working with. This is where the counselor is often very useful in helping to address and assimilate the issues in question with the family. The spirit world also communicates much faster than we do and they will give me information much faster than I can actually deliver it. So they will give me information in spurts, with just enough time for me to deliver the messages before giving me more. For me, it is sort of like listening to what some one is saying to me very quickly in Spanish and then turning around as a translator would do, and telling another in English, much more slowly, what they have said. I am basically a translator or messenger for the spirit world. It is really as simple as that.

The sprits constantly remind me that the way in which a message is delivered has a lot to do with the way in which, and how well it is received. Their job is to give me the messages, my job is to deliver the message in a way that each individual can accept and receive it, while at the same time, taking into consideration and adjusting for, any limiting religious and intellectual beliefs or conditioning that the person may hold or have been raised with.

the messenger

As I mentioned earlier, this night produced a perfect example of a loved one on the spirit side, making sure that his loved one's were going to get their message whether they wanted to or not. It is a story that I remember vividly.

A very attractive blonde haired, middle-aged woman sits on a chair in front of me and to my right. She is dressed conservatively and in very good taste, giving the impression by her visual presentation, that she is likely a woman of some means. Her hair, nails and make-up are all done with great attention to detail, but I would not say over-done. Next to her to her left, is a very good-looking and tall young man with blonde hair, golden sun tanned skin and blue eyes. I estimate he must be about six feet, two inches and he seems all the more tall walking in next to the petite woman who I have already deduced must be his mother. I will later find out in the reading that he is indeed her son and he is twenty-eight-years old.

As I give my usual prep speech to the group, I am very aware of his eyes, which are very intently focused on me. He is studying me and I know that he is the skeptic that the spirits warned me about. I am also aware that he does not know what to make of the fact that he is surprised to see that I am attractive, "normal" looking, and much younger than what he had expected. I am definitely *not* what he had imagined. Although I am quite certain he had no idea what to expect, I obviously don't fit into any of his preconceived ideas of what a medium should look like. I actually get quite a kick out of this, am amused by his thoughts and am now looking forward to reading for him. I always love a good challenge and there is nothing more rewarding to me than to totally blow the mind of a skeptic.

In stark contrast, his mother feels to me very open and hopeful, as if she is looking forward to her reading. She will be much easier to read for because of this. It is obvious to me that her son's energy is very protective and I know that he has come to do just that and protect his mother from me, from being taken for a ride and from disappointment. When Jane calls me the next day, after speaking with the mother and son following the group, she validates that my suspicions were accurate. I know that he does not believe in me or that this whole thing is possible. When his mother told him that I was coming to her grief support group tonight, he became quite worried about her and her state of mind, which to him was obviously now in question. He came along with her, not with the intention of seeing if I was real, because he already knew, of course, that I wasn't – but to protect his mom.

I pivot in my chair and turn to my right so that I am facing both of them; they are the last reading of the group that evening.

"Do you have a brother and son passed?" I ask, looking at the both of them.

"Yes" the mother replies.

I look at her son, "He is telling me that you two are twins, are you twins, identical twins?"

He raises his eyebrows, nods and replies "Yes, yes we are."

"He is telling me that he passed in a car accident, is that correct?"

"Yes"

"He is showing me a road somewhere in what looks like to me, to be out in the country. I believe in the north eastern part of the country, New Jersey or New York area somewhere I think. It is two lanes and winds around through the woods and it is not mountainous, but it is rather hilly. It is night time and he is telling me that it was around one or two a.m. when he crashed. Is this all correct so far?"

His brother is staring intently at me at this point, leaning forward in his chair, he simply nods yes. "It was New Jersey, actually." He is still not convinced, but I am beginning to get his attention now. "He is telling me that road was wet, slick after the rain, it had been raining. He had a few drinks but I would not say he feels like he was drunk, but maybe a little tired. He is the only one in the car and driving. He is showing me from his point of view in the car and I can see the road take a pretty sharp curve to the left and as he hits the curve the back wheels of the car slide out and fish tail. I see the car going off the right side of the road at the sharpest point of the curve, he was going too fast, the road was wet and he misses the turn. Does this all sound like what you know about that night?"

They both are silent and just nod yes.

"He shows me the car rolling over several times, as it rolls off the side of the road and down a sloped embankment." I turn to look directly at his mom. "He wants you to know he passed instantly, his neck snapped. He did not feel anything." His mom starts weeping quietly, tears are running down her face. "He says you need to hear that because they did not find his car until the next morning and you had always worried that he had lay there all night in pain and dying. You were afraid he was trapped in the car. He is telling me the car looked like a crumpled piece of tin foil. He says he wants you to know it was quick. He was out of his body before he even realized what had happened. He also wants you to know that your father, his grandpa came there to meet him."

the messenger

Her emotions are now like a damn breaking and I can see the relief on her face along with the stream of tears running down her cheeks.

"I am so sorry to go through all of these details about the accident with you again, but it is important that you know, so that you know it is really him. I am not allowed to edit any messages that I am given." I explain to both of them. "He is telling me that he was at the house with you when the sheriff came and knocked on the door. He is so sorry about that, he said it was horrible for you. He says the sheriff explained to you that just before the sun came up around six a.m. or so, someone driving by saw the head lights coming out of the trees and called it in."

At this point the brother in spirit, who I will call Paul, is now standing behind me and speaking into my right ear. I find this to be very unusual because spirits will usually stand in front of me and behind their loved ones. Paul is very handsome like his brother and I am becoming aware that he has a very good sense of humor. He is speaking to me now and joking and teasing me, he says to me "*My brother wants proof. This will get him! Tell him that....*"

I turn to look directly at his brother and say "Paul is telling me that you have his wallet in your pocket right now and that it even has all of his things and his money still in it. He is telling me there is a gold poker chip inside of it that he kept from the trip to Vegas you both went on together. He kept the chip for good luck. Do you have his wallet with you now?"

In that moment everything shifted, his brother's jaw practically dropped to the floor and his face turned white as if he had actually seen a ghost. He slowly stood up without saying a word and reached into his back pocket to pull out his brother's wallet, with all of his things still in it, even the money and most importantly; the poker chip which he pulls out of the wallet to show us all in the group! I was just as stunned as he was

Every spirit communicates with me differently, some show me pictures and images and it is like we are playing charades. Some will impress me with feelings and emotions, while others will quite literally speak to me in thoughts. Paul was one who showed me images, but also he spoke to me and I could hear his words as clearly as I heard his mom and brother's. In fact, it was really amazing how well he communicated with me.

His brother took a moment to compose himself and began to tell me that before he picked his mother up, he put the wallet in his pocket. He told me that on the drive over to pick her up, he spoke out loud to his brother and said. "Paul, if this is really you tonight, if this is really real, then I want you to tell me about the wallet."

His mother was stunned, she looked at me and said, "I had no idea he had done that," and then looked back at her son in shock. Her face was filled with excitement not only for the proof that is was really Paul, but that she knew how much this had just impacted her living son.

Paul continues on to tell me, "Now tell them this..." he said.

Looking at his brother, I ask "Paul wants me to ask, do you remember when you and your brother were dating the two sisters just after high school and you decided to pretend you were the other brother for one night so you could switch dates?"

He immediately starts laughing and blushing and replies a little embarrassed and shaking his head back and forth in disbelief "Yes, we did do that.".

His mother puts her hands to her face and I can see she is about to burst with excitement, I look at her, obviously waiting for her to share what it is that has her so excited.

"Well, when I was waiting at home for my son to pick me up, I was sitting with Paul's picture in my hands on the couch and I asked out loud to Paul, I said "Paul, if it is really you tonight, then I want you tell that very same story about you and your brother. That is just incredible, absolutely amazing!!! I cannot believe he came through with that. Wow!"

Now mind you, there are six other people in the group, as well as Jane, witnessing this reading. Not only did he bring through information that I could never have known, he also brought things through that there was no way Jane could have even known before the reading. Just in case there was still any doubt on his brother's part, that Jane and I were working together and she was feeding me information, the details that he brought through were brought to dismiss that suspicion. Again, I was just as amazed as everyone there that night and could hardly believe the words coming out of my own mouth. The reading continued on for about thirty more minutes as Paul brought through a lot more specific and detailed information about a family business that he, his brother, and their dad all ran together. He even gave his brother some advice on how to handle some very specific issues that were currently going on in the business. He also told me that their father would never do something like this, go to a medium, he would never believe this. His brother and mother laughed and nodded in agreement.

Paul had a great sense of humor and kept everyone laughing all night, including his brother and mom. He ended the evening with such an upbeat and positive feeling that I am certain everyone there that night was on a high for days after.

the messenger

Paul knew his brother and mom were suffering greatly and struggling to come to terms with his sudden and tragic passing. He also knew that they needed proof, especially his brother, to be able to believe that it was really him and he did a great job of bringing through things that only they would have known. Paul also proved to them that night that he was, in no uncertain terms, alive and well and still carried with him the same great charm and sense of humor he had in his life. He also showed them that he was still around them by bringing through the things they asked him too and talking about things that had happened with their business that occurred after his passing.

The mother and brother gave me big hugs before they left that night and thanked me. And, about a week later, after they had time to really absorb it all, the mother wrote me a wonderful letter thanking me again. I know that they will always miss Paul and be sad that he left them so early, but I also know that that night changed their lives forever. That night changed the way they viewed his life and death, and his life after death. For they know now, that he is indeed alive and well and never really far away and all they have to do is think of him and he is there with them.

> "I received this letter shortly after the first printing of the book. Due to the confidentiality and annonymity policy of the Grief Group I was working with at the time, I was never told Jason's or his Mom's names when I had read for them. I had no way of contacting him to let him know about the story in the book. I was so happy when I received this letter from Jason only a few weeks after my book was first released. I felt it really needed to be shared with the story and the reader. Jason and his brother Eric will always hold a special place in my heart." (edited and added Sept 2011 after First Printing*) - Denise

February 18, 2010,

"I wanted to back up the story you have all read here today. This story was about my mother and I. The man killed in the accident was Eric Hayes. I was truly shocked with events of the evening. Denise was right in saying that I was a skeptic about the whole thing and wanted to make sure my mother was ok. I did however leave there with a new found calmness in my heart and I think the evenings events erased years of potential therapy. I just wanted to thank you Denise! What you do really helps people in their time of need and I am honored that my story stuck out it your memory. I hope this story will give a breath of hope to others in their time of need!"

Thanks again!
Jason Hayes

Chapter 7
Happiness is No Tan Lines and a Tropical Tan

Happiness is No Tan Lines and a Tropical Tan

I am as surprised as anyone by the work that I currently do as a professional medium with grief groups and I did not grow up thinking I wanted to be a professional psychic. In fact, I would say that I actually went to great lengths to try and avoid this work and keep it a secret.

The environment that I grew up in was not supportive of my unique vision of the world and my sense of "knowing." I did not even tell anyone for thirty-four years that I could see and hear spirits – not a soul. In addition to my mom becoming an extremely religious Christian fundamentalist, it is important to note that my biological father spent the majority of his adult life being hospitalized in mental health institutions. He was diagnosed with schizophrenia because he was quite convinced that he heard voices and saw people that others believed were not really there. He lived a very tortured existence of isolation, heavy medications and shock treatment therapy which led to his suicide after he was eventually released from institutional life. So, I grew up with a very real concern that if I told my family that I saw and heard people that no one else could see, they would not believe me, would think that I was mentally ill like my father, and have me committed too.

It was widely believed that schizophrenia may have a hereditary factor and the doctors had even spoken to my mother about that fact when I was very young. I did vaguely allude with my mom about my psychic abilities a few times over the years, like my ability to just know things before they happened but she quickly sent me some biblical verses from the Old

Testament that implied that these abilities were from Satan and his trickery and then told me that I should "abstain." In other words, she wanted me to "just say no" to my abilities. I found that idea to be incredibly ridiculous. It would be like asking me to ignore her or my husband, if they were standing right in front of me and to pretend that I could not see them or hear them– like they were not really there and not real. Yeah right, that was not possible. My mother to this day firmly believes that what I do is wrong according to the Bible, against God and refuses to acknowledge or even discuss any aspect of what I do. This fact has made my personal journey in this life quite difficult and painful over the years and is still a source of contention and division in my relationship with my family of origin.

So, being the very independent and adventurous person that I am, I left home as soon as I could at the ripe age of nineteen. When I went to college, I pursued studies in the visual arts, philosophy, psychology, anthropology, sociology, ancient civilizations and physics trying to learn anything I could about my abilities, the spirit world, world beliefs, and how energy worked in the physical world.

In college while my friends were partying and doing the usual college things I was reading books about near death experiences and hauntings. After graduation, I decided to pursue my more creative interests which led me in many career directions, but always as an entrepreneur, providing services for people.

My knack for knowing things about people, future events and trends, made being successful in whatever business I pursued quite easy and fun. I found ways to put my abilities to work to help people and deliver important messages from the spirit world, covertly and under the cover of the businesses that I owned.

I was always aware of my true purpose here, even if people around me had no idea. I considered myself to be a "secret agent for the greater good," kind of like a spiritual social worker who helped people at pivotal points in their life to stay on, or get back on track with their own individual life purpose. I always like to say if God had a satellite office here on earth, where we could check in when we were not sure which direction to go, I would be like the guidance counselor that looks over your course work and personal file and helps you decide what to do next. Metaphorically speaking, I can pick up the "phone" and call the spirit world and check in with your planners on the other side and see what directions they may have for you.

the messenger

Over the years, I became very good at delivering messages and information to people stealthily through well-timed suggestions and skillful advice. I did this in a way that would insure they had no idea where the message was coming from, but all the while, I could still get the messages through that the sprits wanted delivered.

Eventually my entrepreneurial career led me down the path of opening and operating the day spa. I acquired a cosmetologist license which allowed me to perform spa services, as well as, a personal training license which enabled me to help people not only look better on the outside, but also become healthier from the inside. The combination of the two put me in close one-on-one contact with a large number of people and build a large clientele that I helped multi-dimensionally. It was the perfect fit because it allowed me to advise, coach and encourage people in whatever way they needed. People also always felt comfortable confiding in me their most intimate details and concerns in life, which further allowed me the opening to bring through the messages that the spirit world really needed them to know. It did not matter to me if they knew where the message was coming from – whether it was from me or from their mother who was passed over – it only mattered that they got the message.

I enjoyed my work at the spa and also as a personal trainer at my husband's martial arts studio and gym. It was a great combination and the perfect platform for my undercover work for the spirit world. I was quite happy and comfortable with the behind the scenes role that I played and really had no desire to leave it or be out in the open about who I really was and what I really did. Spirit, however, had different plans for me as I was soon to find out.

You see, I actually work for them…and as with any employer, they decide where I am needed and best put to use. So, I have learned to be flexible and open to change, because I have learned that when they say it is time for me to make a move I'd better be ready to go.

…*As a lot of people sometimes do in life, I eventually reached a mid-life point where I began to question everything about my life, who I was sharing it with, what I was doing and why. It was be a time of great turmoil and complete upheaval. Not only did I question everything about it, I questioned my own abilities, the spirit world and even God for a time.*

It was at this very pivotal point in my life that everything quite suddenly changed a full 360 degrees. It is also around this time that I met William and his son Walter.

Key West, with its eclectic, diverse and quirky inhabitants and visitors, is a very fun and interesting place to live and work. Let's just say there is never a dull moment and plenty of real life entertainment to go around. My day spa and tanning salon are no different and provide the perfect back-drop for the never ending cast of characters that call Key West home. The tanning salon is located in the heart of downtown "Old Town" Key West right on Duval Street and features the most interesting cross section of the residents in Key West. I have enjoyed many years of sitting behind the counter of the small tanning salon, greeting my regular clients and listening to all of their sorted tales about their lives in Key West. The counter is set up in the style of a bar, with a few bar stools around it and features cocktails of tanning lotions and oils instead of liquor. As you walk in the door the counter is directly in front, the waiting area is on the right with couches and chairs, and the individual tanning rooms lined up behind that. The signature colors of the tanning salon and day spa are yellow and orange. Both locations are painted Caribbean style with alternating yellow and orange walls and trim, and are decorated with a variety of sun's that I have collected over the years either in my travels or which have been given to me by my clients. The colors and décor reflect the names of the two locations, Tropical Tan and The Solar Spa. I discovered rather early on with the tanning salon, that many of the clients enjoy hanging out in there as much as they do tanning, so, it is not unusual for my regular clients, who visit the salon several days a week, to hang around for a while before or after their appointments. They stay just to talk and I have come to know them all very well and intimately. Many of them I have grown quite frond of and attached too.

Most are adventurous types; artistic, creative – generally non-conformists – the types of people that I like most. They move to Key West for varied reasons, from places all over the world, although a few are native born. Many make the move to Key West in search of finding who they are, others move to escape who they were, some have come because of the water and the relaxed lifestyle, while others come just for the party. Quite a few are social dropouts, outcasts, and the protestors of dogma, traditional life styles and societal roles. They come to Key West looking for acceptance, tolerance and the freedom to just be who they are without judgment.

The residents of Key West are all connected by a common thread that keeps this place a very tightly knit, and harmonious community. For all of its diversity and character, Key West is a very peaceful place to live. There

the messenger

is very little violent crime, with most of the crime centered around the party front initiating arrests for public drunkenness, public nudity, petty theft or small-time drug infractions. The crime report in the *Key West Citizen* is typically read for its comedic factor more than anything else. It is quite likely that whoever is featured in the crime report, is probably someone that you know, as every one in Key West knows just about everyone else. Everyone here also knows what everyone else is up to. Key West has all the gossip and interconnectedness enjoyed by the residents of any small town in America, while at the same time; it is mixed with the cultural and social diversity of a big city like Manhattan. But for the most part, the residents have adopted a live and let live policy of tolerance and acceptance that makes it a very special place to live with the freedom to just be who you are.

The clientele of the tanning salon on Duval Street boasts a lively cast of characters, many of whom work the night shift, or enjoy the night life, and sleep during the day. Most of them have very diverse occupations including folks that work in the souvenir and t-shirt shops downtown, small business owners, bartenders, waiters, male and female strippers as well as, a few lawyers and city politicians who work at the court house nearby. There are even a well known male escort, members of a local rock cover band and a few locally famous Drag Queens. I can tell you just about anything about anyone in town after sitting at the counter of the tanning salon all these years. I hear it all!

My second spa, The Solar Spa, is located on the other side of the island and has quite a different vibe and clientele. In addition to tanning beds, the spa offers all the usual comforts and luxuries. The north side of the island, called "New Town" is less transient than the downtown or "Old Town" crowd. The schools, ball fields, grocery stores and meager strip-style shopping centers are located on this side of paradise. Many of the residents on this side of the island are the business owners, bankers and professionals and this is where most families inhabit the island. The "Conch's" also live mostly in New Town. "Conch" is a coveted title given only to the residents born and raised in Key West, with many of the families going back four generations or more. Most are of Cuban heritage and are the backbone of Key West's rich and colorful history which includes; the fishing and seafood industry, treasure salvaging, bootlegging during prohibition and even piracy just a century ago.

When I first moved to Key West, I worked on a dive and snorkel boat where I met my first husband, my son's father, who was a sport fisherman. It was through him that I met some of the older Conch's that worked on the docks and on the shrimp and fishing boats. At the end of the day, I would sit and wait for his boat to come in with their catch and while I waited, the old timers would tell me stories of how many of them had spent time in jail for smuggling marijuana into Everglades City on the mainland back in the seventies and eighties.

The clientele at the Spa, although equally interesting and diverse, is not quite as edgy and socially deviant as the downtown crowd. Many of my colleagues in the Rotary Club and Chamber of Commerce, come to this spa. Javier's Gym and Martial Arts School is located on this side of the island just behind the spa and down Kennedy Drive about a mile or so. Since I opened the spa four years ago, I don't spend much time downtown at the tanning salon. My days are split between running the spa and doing services and personal training my clients at the gym and helping Javier with the martial arts school.

This week is particularly busy as it is the kick-off of the week-long Fantasy Fest celebration on the island. The tanning beds will be going non-stop and I am booked solid for three days, waxing my clients and removing all of their unwanted body hair. They do this before they adorn their scantily clad bodies with body paint, costumes, beads and other decorative apparel in preparation for all the week's festivities. Fantasy Fest is similar to Mardi Gras in New Orleans or Carnival in Brazil, but on a smaller scale. It is a sight to behold and quite an eye-opening experience for first timers. The kick off weekend, the Goombay Festival, is always the weekend before Halloween and is held downtown in the heart of Old Town, in Bahama Village. Bahama Village is just as it sounds, a quaint neighborhood made of a few blocks of Bahamian style cottages as the original residents were originally of Bahamian and Haitian decent. The architecture is charming, tropical and colorful as one might imagine. Goombay is more an event for the locals than the tourists. The street fair lasts all weekend and features a variety of live music and dancing in the streets with lots of fresh seafood, Caribbean and Cuban food. There are street vendors offering a wide array of handmade arts and crafts, street performers, fortune tellers, and of course, lots of tropical drinks to go around.

The following week is filled with parades, costume contests, Hemingway look-alike contests, pet costume contests, pet parades, body paint contests (a big favorite), tattoo contests, tea dances and drag shows. We even

the messenger

have a bed race where people push a bed on wheels and an occupant wearing pajamas down Duval Street. The week ends with a big party and parade on Duval Street Saturday night the week of Halloween. For the most part, everyone on the island participates one way or another in the festivities. It is the ultimate in adult fun and silliness – a no holds barred, week of uninhibited fun, play and fantasy. For me, it means the spa and the tanning salon will be very busy with people anxious to have tanned skin and polished nails beneath their customary skimpy costumes.

Today I am driving into the spa first thing this morning to take care of a few things before I head over to the gym to train my Tuesday/Thursday afternoon clients. Javier's Gym & Studio is small but sufficient for him to train his clients and teach classes. He teaches a full schedule of classes in the morning and the evenings of Tae Kwon Do, Jui Jitsu and Kickboxing and in the afternoons, he also trains clients privately. Some are there for conditioning and exercise while others are there to be coached for mixed Martial Arts competitions. Today he is training Walter privately one to one in kickboxing. Walter is the son of my one o'clock weight training client William.

Walter is in his last year of college in Boston and is in town with some college buddies for the festivities and to visit his dad. He is a good-looking young man with a thin but athletic build, dark hair and striking blue eyes. He is charming, self assured, flirtatious and slightly cocky. It is not difficult to see why he is so self assured. He comes from a very wealthy family and is thoroughly enjoying his privileged social stature. He knows that once out of college he will be mentored by his dad to eventually be a captain of industry and he will inherit his father's massive business empire. His good looks, charm and silver spoon also make him quite attractive to the ladies and a most eligible bachelor. He is young, in his prime and enjoying life as any young man in his shoes would do. Although I have been training his dad for about six months now, and have heard all about him and his sister, this is the first time I have met Walter.

William is a challenging client. I like him, but like many men who aspire to such high levels of success, his personal life has suffered greatly for it and he has paid a heavy price with his health. William is fifty-nine but looks easily ten years older. I can see in his facial features his son's good looks and can imagine William was also once quite handsome when he was younger and in better shape. He has come to me on the advice and encouragement of his doctor. He is in the midst of his third divorce from a much younger woman and it is proving to be very nasty and contentious from what he tells me.

I have learned a great deal about William over the past six months, He was married to Walter's mother for fourteen years, the longest of any of the three wives. He is a tall man at six feet, four inches and according to his doctor, is about eighty pounds overweight. His blood pressure is too high, his cholesterol is off the charts, he smokes and drinks too much and in spite of living in the lap of material luxury, he seems to be very stressed most of the time. It seems that staying at the top of the game is even more stressful than getting there.

We talk a lot about changing his diet, eating healthier and drinking less, but I know my words fall on deaf ears. He is a man with many vices and addictions and seems to consistently peg the needle in every area of his life. The primary focus of his life and journey has exclusively revolved around the pursuit of money, stature and power with everything else falling second. He bought a house in Key West about six months ago, with the intention of starting over and getting away from his troubles. He also wants to do some deep sea fishing which he greatly enjoys. In advance of his son's arrival, he set up the kickboxing training with Javier, for Walter.

I am the first to arrive at the gym and Kelly greets me from the front desk.

"Javier is not back from lunch yet, he went to the Deli. William and Walter are in the back warming up on the treadmills. You're three o'clock called and had to cancel," Kelly continues her on from her list of messages. "She said she is really sorry but some thing has come up and I rescheduled her for Thursday."

"Thanks Kelly, how is it going today? How are you?"

"It's kind of quiet; I guess everyone is downtown at Fantasy Fest. I had Walter fill out the paper work," she hands me the clip board. "He is also scheduled for Thursday with Javier."

"Okay great. You can give this clipboard to Javier when he comes in. I'm going to go in the back and see if William is ready to go." I put my bag in the office and head to the back of the studio towards William and Walter.

"Hi guys", I smile and nod, acknowledging Walter. I extend my hand, "I'm Denise, it's a pleasure to meet you, and William has told me so much about you. Have you been to Fantasy Fest before?"

"Hi, my Dad has told me all about you too. He says with a bit of a smirk.

the messenger

"You have a tough job getting this guy into shape!" he laughs, looking sideways at his dad who is on the treadmill next to him. I came down with some friends from school, none of us have been to Fantasy fest before but we are ready to rock!" he says with a big grin.

He is definitely charming and a little flirtatious and I am aware he is checking me out. I am told that I look about ten years younger than I am, and I am feeling like he must think I am much younger and closer to his age than I actually am.

"Okay William are you ready?" I say, as I motion him towards the bench press machine. "See you later Walter, have fun. Javier should be here any minute."

As I begin William's workout, I glance up to see if Javier has arrived yet and see that Walter is watching us. We make brief eye contact; he smiles and nervously looks away as if he had been caught "looking." I smile and continue talking to William.

After that day, I would not see Walter again until the spring. William continued to train with me pretty regularly when he was in town. He has a private jet, and upon the advice of his doctor has recently taken measures to relax and enjoy his life of luxury a bit more by taking some time off to vacation and travel. He has been bitten by the deep sea fishing bug since being in Key West, and has begun to passionately pursue the ever elusive Sail Fish and Blue Marlin that migrate through the waters of the keys in winter, by way of the Gulf Stream. He is out of town a lot of the time traveling to Costa Rica, Mexico and Cuba in pursuit of big fish. When he is in town, he comes to workout with me and we pass the time by swapping fishing stories. He keeps me entertained with stories of the fish that did and didn't get away. I have done quite a lot of deep sea and bill-fishing over the years with my fist husband who was a sport fisherman. I have never been much of a fisherman myself, but I probably know more about salt water fishing, bait, lures and tackle than most recreational anglers and I have always enjoyed going along as a spectator. So I was an eager listener to Williams' tales.

I met my first husband in Key West when I was working on a catamaran taking snorkeler's to the reef. His boat was docked next to mine. He took people out on a 54' Hatteras Deep Sea fishing boat off the coast of Key West. I have had the fortunate opportunity of seeing fish and ocean life that most Anglers only dream of seeing. I have been on the boat to see more times than I can count, such world record fish being caught as a Blue Marlin over 400lbs, countless Sail Fish, White Marlins, Hammerhead sharks, Giant Bull sharks, Dolphin, Tuna and every other fish species that migrates through the keys. I have been aboard the boat when we have come upon pods of whales and dolphins that came so close to the boat that they swam and played in its wake. I have been aboard for many fishing tournaments and have braved weather and seas of as much as 14 ft, as the Hatteras bobbed back and forth like a cork in the sea. I must say it is quite an amazing site to see a 450lb Blue Marlin fight on a line for an hour or more, jumping up and sailing through the air several feet and then being brought right up to the side of the boat where it's released back into the sea. I easily recall that his eye was the size of my head and his massive size and impressive strength were nothing less than astonishing. It is impossible to forget the beauty and intensity of the colors of its skin as the fish lights up with excitement. Rich rainbows of deep blue, green and turquoise glow within the shiny sleek texture of its thin leathery skin. I can see why people get quite literally addicted to fishing. I used to think with my first husband that fishing was much like an addiction really.

I would say, "How can you sit there all day long, day after day, in the hot sun, sometimes going all day or hours not catching a fish? I would never have the patience for that!"

He would reply, "Because you never know when you're gonna get that big bite. You're just waiting for that one bite…the big one!" and his eyes would light up just talking about it he would get so excited and impassioned. Just like a gambler I thought to myself, just waiting to hit the big one!

Chapter 8
Revolution, Chaos & Revelation... In That Order

the messenger

Revolution, Chaos & Revelation... In That Order

It was interesting timing when I met William. I had just recently divorced about a year and a half earlier. Javier and I had been dating for about six months when I started training William. It was a difficult time for me personally and professionally. I was questioning everything about my life at that time. As divorces go, I would say that mine was not too bad and more amicable than most. However, we certainly had our share of struggles, arguing over our stuff and child custody. We had had a beautiful home together right on the water. As any person who has been through a divorce knows, it is very a very difficult process separating two adjoining lives to start over. It can also be financially devastating in many cases, as was mine. Too make financial matters worse the events of 9-11 happened only three months after my divorce. People were very afraid after that time to travel or fly and tourism everywhere came to a screeching halt for many months. Key West, being a community with an economy that survives primarily on the influx of tourist dollars, was practically immobilized in the months that followed 9-11. I struggled to stay afloat with my businesses and as tourism stopped, so did my revenues because my clients all worked in jobs or businesses that survived on tourist dollars. I watched the value of my businesses plummet, while at the same time my debts increased exponentially. I borrowed money to try to maintain them and just keep up with the day to day expenses. As the country was gripped by fear and indecision, I watched my assets quickly turn into liabilities and wondered how long I could survive and how long the downturn would last. I watched every thing that I had built for the past ten years, both professionally and personally, slowly begin to crumble around me – my family, my business, my life. I was mentally exhausted and emotionally devastated.

It was a very confusing time in my life, but now as I look back, I see it as the most productive and a real turning point for me. I learned a lot and I learned it quickly. I learned that the human spirit can survive and thrive even amidst and after great tragedy and loss. I discovered what I was really made of and found out I was more courageous, resourceful and resilient than I had realized.

But, it was also a time that I became very disenchanted with my gifts and abilities. I was just beginning to understand how they worked, but was still confused as to how they applied to me and my own personal life. I became frustrated and even angry with the spirit world and God. I could not begin to comprehend how things could have gone so terribly wrong in my life – how I could have made such a mess of it all. I could not understand why I could see everyone else's future and help them on their journey but not see any of this coming in my own life. I felt like I had been blindsided and it all seemed to me like one big cruel joke which just happened to be on me. I had always followed my intuition and my hunches and I always believed in them but for the first time, I was not so sure. I had real doubts about the trustworthiness of my instincts and the guidance that Spirit had given me all my life. After all, this was not how things in my life were supposed to have turned out; this is not what I wanted. I did not deserve this!

So, for the first time in my life I swore off the spirit world and all of my gifts. By just word of mouth, I had been giving readings to friends and clients for years. I regularly read for many of my clients and employees and anyone who knew me well, new about my abilities. I read with Tarot cards back then and it would often be while I was giving a card reading that someone from the spirit side, usually a parent or loved one, would take the opportunity to stop in and say "Hi" to the loved one that I was reading for. I was still not telling many people about my ability to see and hear spirits, but I was rather open about reading the cards. I would just sort of play it down as a fun thing and it was a great way to connect with people.

In my state of frustration and deep despair, I told my friends and helpers on the spirit side, "That's it, I'm done with this! I'm not doing this anymore for anyone. Why should I use my gifts to help anyone else when I cannot even use them to help myself? It's not fair. It's also too confusing and I am going to stick with what makes sense and the real world."

the messenger

I was also inwardly questioning if I should even be advising anyone else based on these abilities when I was currently questioning their validity and credibility myself. So, I put the cards away and became determined to only navigate through my life in a rational and logical manner just like everyone else did. Whenever I saw spirits or sensed them, I asked them to go away and leave me alone. I made it clear that I was going to start doing things my way and on my own terms and that I no longer wanted any of their help. So they did, they left me alone, for a little while – until I saw Walter again.

Just about a week before William walked back into the gym and my life, I reluctantly agreed to do a reading for Kelly the gym's front desk clerk. I had come in late one morning to find her terribly distraught over the recent break-up from her long time boyfriend. She was crying and very emotional. I had never read for her before, but she had heard through several of my clients and employees about my readings. Her mother had very recently passed and she was anxious to speak with her too. I had not really announced to anyone that I was no longer giving readings; it was really more of a personal pact between me and my spirit friends. Although I really did not want to read for her, I found it very difficult to refuse Kelly. She seemed to be in such a distressed state and at the same time she was talking to me, I was aware of her mother being there with us standing behind her, so I reluctantly agreed to meet her at her house later that afternoon. I did not bring my cards as I knew the reading would be to connect with her mom and since I was already connected with her, the cards were really unnecessary. In actuality, I really did not need the cards at all anymore and hadn't for quite some time. I had only continued to use them because people had become accustomed to them and had come to expect me to give them a card reading.

Kelly's house was downtown on Von Phister, which was one of my favorite streets in Key West. It featured some of the most beautiful homes on the island located in a lush, tropical, setting by The Casa Marina resort. Her house was tidy and quaint, decorated in hues of yellow and green with oriental décor. It was made complete by a pair of pet Siamese cats. We sat down in the living room and it barely took me a minute to connect with her mom and start with the reading.

"Your mother is here, but first before we speak with her there is someone else here too. I cannot get around him so I would like to try and identify him and bring him through first, so that then I can get on to your mother. He is very insistent. He is a young man and good looking from what I can tell, with dark hair and my guess looks to be around twenty-two or twenty-four. He is just not very clear to me. I can just barely make him out. For some reason, it is hard for me to see him…it is almost like I am looking at him through static, like on a TV screen. He is very upset and is telling me he was shot. Do you know who this is? He is still earthbound and has not crossed over yet like your mom has, he is here, standing right there…" I say as I point to the south east corner of the living room. "I feel like he has not been passed long, maybe a few weeks."

Kelly shakes her head, thinking, but she is unable to make the connection. "I don't know," she says, shrugging her shoulders and still shaking her head.

"He says his name is "Walt….Walter? He says that you know him, he is very upset and kind of pacing around the room."

Still shaking her head back and forth with a very puzzled look, Kelly says "I have no idea who he is" and neither did I – nothing was clicking for me.

"Well you know what, hold on to this. I have been doing this a long time and I have learned that sooner or later something will click and you will figure out who he is. Let me know when you do." He then vanished and I was able to move on to her mother.

I went on to finish her reading connecting with her mom, dad and grandmother, but I left her house with both of us puzzled over who Walter was.

It wasn't until spring and exactly one week after my reading for Kelly when I saw William again. I had not trained him in almost four months, and actually I had not seen nor heard from him at all since then as he was leaving for Costa Rica the last time I saw him just before Christmas

It was March and peak season, Javier and I were both busy as were our businesses. I was having a weird week, is the best way I can describe it. I was just not feeling up to par and my usual upbeat and energetic self. I couldn't quite put my finger on why – I was just feeling kind of tired and a little depressed for no apparent reason. I had also been feeling anxious and worrying about all sorts of things which was not usually in my nature to do. To further irritate my mood and add to my distress, it seemed like all the technology around me had gone haywire this week. The computer in my office at the spa, as well as, my computer at home seemed to both have gotten some sort of a virus or something that was causing them both to turn on and off randomly. It also kept causing the screen to get grainy and unclear and somewhat staticy. I had tried everything I could think of

the messenger

to fix them both, including running virus and diagnostics software. But I continually came up with nothing. My son was even complaining about it when he would use our computer at home. He seemed to be having the same issues. This had been going on for close to a week when just this morning I went into the bathroom and turned on the light and it literally exploded in its socket. It took me fifteen minutes to get what was left of the bulb out of the socket as it had nearly been welded into the threads. The lights had been flickering in the house for several days so I assumed we must be having some power surges which were common in Key West from time to time.

On top of it all I was sure that I must be coming down with something, a cold or the flu, because this morning out of the blue I suddenly felt nauseas and threw-up in the bathroom. I just felt like I was in a funk, just tired, depressed and generally having a difficult time coping with life all week. Again, this is not at all my usual demeanor. Javier had come over the night before only to find me on the couch in tears with no explanation of why I was feeling so sad. I just could not stop crying. The nausea passed as quickly as it came so I felt safe to go into work. I had a full day of clients to train at the gym and I really didn't want to call everyone to cancel at the last minute, so I mustered up the strength and headed to the gym. I figured at the very least, seeing my client's was sure to improve my mood.

I was training a client, Teri when William walked in. I was on my knees with my hands on Teri's feet, holding them steady, as I counted her crunches.

"Okay 5 more, you're almost done. Come on you can do it....three...two....one! Great, we're done for today. See you on Thursday." I looked up just as William walked over.

"Hey William, what's up? Where have you been? I haven't seen you in awhile," I said to him. Thinking he had just arrived back in town and had come in to set up his training sessions, I was expecting to hear all about his latest adventure on the high seas. What he told me next, was not something that I was at all prepared to hear. I later found out the story had been in the *Key West Citizen* about three weeks earlier, but I had not seen it and had no knowledge of it at all.

He dropped the bomb. "Yeah, well I have been out of town for awhile and I just got back this week. I have been in New York. Walter's funeral was last week."

Confused by his statement, I quickly scanned my memory for who Walter was. I thought of his son briefly, but immediately dismissed the thought as his son was only twenty-four. So I assumed he must have been talking about someone else. I was still confused and had not yet made the connection when he continues.

"I can't believe it," he says shaking his head back and forth. "I just bought a condo in Fort Lauderdale a few months ago that we were going to move into together after he graduated in June. "*Walt*" was looking forward to it. "*Walter*" and I were going to start a new business together."

Just then everything clicked! "*Walt…Walter*," just as I had heard the names in Kelly's reading last week. Oh my God, I thought to myself and it all hit me suddenly like a freight train - *I got it!* My mind flashed back to the reading I did for Kelly at her house. I was speechless - dumbfounded, shocked, and in complete disbelief! I had just seen Walter – Javier had trained him only a few months ago.

"Oh my God, William…I am so sorry. What happened?"

"He was shot, in downtown Boston. I guess he and some friends were heading out on a Friday night to hit the nightclubs. He was going to graduate in two months." Walter looks down to the floor.

What do you say in these moments? It is hard to imagine – to comprehend the intensity of pain that William was dealing with. I struggled for words.

"Oh William, I am so sorry. If there is any thing you need, anything Javier and I can do for you, please do not hesitate to ask – anything at all," I repeated.

"Thanks, I just wanted to let you know why you haven't heard from me in awhile. There was an investigation and we could not lay him to rest and have services for several weeks. I guess it's been about a month now since he was killed. I am heading back to New York for awhile. His mother, as you can imagine is not doing well. I'm not sure when I'll be back. I just came to take care of a few things here. I'm leaving Monday."

"Okay William," I said still in disbelief as William turned and walked to the door. I couldn't move. I was stunned, immobilized actually. The gym was empty except for Kelly who was reading a magazine at the front desk. I walked into my office, closed the door and sat down. My mind raced as I was flooded with memories and information. It was all making sense now, all coming back to me – the reading with Kelly and Walter. He was trying to come through to Kelly and me. He knew I was going to see his dad and he wanted to get a message through to him. The lights flickering in the house, the light bulb exploding, the computers turning on and off, my feelings of being depressed, sad and overwhelmed all week, the nausea – it all made

the messenger

sense now. He was trying to get through to me and he was still earthbound, he had not yet crossed over.

Walter was the first earthbound spirit that I had seen and spoken with, so it was no wonder I was so confused all week. Until this point, I had only connected with spirits who were crossed over and on the spirit side of life, but Walter was still here in the physical world. He was sad, scared and distraught so his energy level was very low and on a very low frequency which explained why I was having a hard time getting a clear picture of him and why he seemed to be in "static" when he came through to me in Kelly's reading.

I have always been very strongly clairsentient, which means that spirits can impress on me physical and emotional feelings and sensations. I quickly realized that the depression and feelings of overwhelming sadness – had been his feelings, not mine. The nausea that I had experienced had been the result of absorbing so much of Walter's energy and feelings of despair and helplessness. His presence in my home all week and the intensity of his emotional state had been draining my own energy to the point of making me physically ill. This was all so new to me, dealing with a spirit who was still on the earth plane. Up to that point, I had not yet learned techniques to protect myself from becoming so connected empathically to a spirit still here on the earth plane and had therefore become drained by the experience.

I got up from my desk, left my office and walked over to Kelly who was sitting at the front desk. I proceeded to tell her what William had just shared with me and how I made the Walter connection to her reading. Her mouth dropped.

"Oh my God that was in the *Citizen* about three weeks ago. I just remembered! I meant to tell you about it and then I completely forgot. Oh my God, I can't believe it! How awful for William," she exclaimed.

"Yes, I know. Apparently Walter was trying to get a message through to us in your reading last week. I just did not recognize him. It was just so hard to get a clear picture of him. Now I understand why."

There was no doubt in mine or Kelly's mind that Walter had come through to both of us in her reading. If I had not had Kelly as a witness to the whole sequence of events I might not have believed it myself. Her validation of me, the information that I had received about Walter during her reading, and then her personal knowledge knowing William and Walter from the gym proved to be invaluable to me.

I have found throughout my lifetime, that with these abilities, the most difficult thing about coming to terms with them has been proving to myself that these experiences are real and trustworthy. For me personally and professionally, this reading was a turning point in my life. I had some doubts myself about how the spirit world worked in my own life. I had wondered on more than one occasion if I might just be crazy or delusional. It is not easy to keep believing in yourself, when most of the people you meet and society tells you that who you are and what you do is not real. Self doubt affects all of us in one way or another and I am no different. This event in my life, however, proved to me in no uncertain terms, that I was not crazy and that this was all very real. What I was experiencing could even be validated and substantiated in the physical world. I had witnesses this time, Kelly, Javier and even Chris had all witnessed the sequence of events at different points. Once I had finally figured out what was going on, the lights in my house stopped flickering and my computer problems ended.

I give Walter some credit for setting me on the course that I'm on today. It was my experience with Walter that proved to me, in no uncertain terms, that I was indeed, not crazy. And, it was his story and personal connection with my life, that finally convinced me that I had a very rare and valuable gift that I needed to honor and share. I realized it would not be right or in accordance with my true purpose in life to stop doing readings.

Once I figured out who Walter was and that he had been hanging around my house all week, I made a naïve and inexperienced decision, which I would almost immediately regret. I decided that I must call William and tell him the story. Now, mind you I had not told many people that I could see and hear spirits. I did not normally make a habit of telling people things that I knew, and I had never before delivered a message to someone who had not come to me for a reading or asked. As a matter of ethics and integrity, I had always felt that it was important for someone to "ask" me to look into their life – giving me permission to do so before I did. In this case however, I felt strongly compelled because I thought that telling William his son was ok and wanted to speak to him, was such a rare opportunity for him to get some answers and closure. I felt that I had too.

So, I called William and told him the whole story about what I could do and why I did not tell people. I told him about Kelly's reading and all the activity that had been occurring in my house. But I knew immediately as the first words came out of my mouth, that I had made a mistake. I knew right away that he did not believe me. He told me that since Walter's death

the messenger

he had received about a half dozen emails from psychics claiming to have messages from his son, hokey psychics who wanted a lot of money and were obviously scanning the obituaries. I offered to come over and read for him and insisted there would be no charge and that I just wanted to help him because I could. He said he would think about it, but I never saw him again after that. Looking back, I should have known that he wouldn't have believed in this sort of thing. He was too pragmatic and a rational thinking businessman. I don't think that I upset him too much, and I surmised that he probably just thought I was a bit nutty, but I learned a very valuable lesson that day; that I would *never* do that again. I would never deliver a message a spirit asked me to, without the person asking me first. Well, almost never. I did go on to deliver one more message like that again and against my better judgment, many years later. I will tell you about that spirit a little later in the story.

As for Walter, well he was the first spirit besides my own grandfather, which I had known in my life and then saw again on the spirit side. Up until meeting Walter, all of the spirits that I had met were always random strangers that I never knew making it relatively easy to maintain a level of detachment from my experiences with the spirit world. This experience had brought everything into a whole new, very personal, light. I went home, focused and sat down to talk to Walter – to find out what happened, why he was still here and what he wanted me to do for him.

Walter was very sad and feeling bad about the decision he had made that put him in the wrong place at the wrong time. He told me that he had gone to downtown Boston with some friends from school to cop some drugs for the weekend. As college kids often do, they were going to a party and were looking for some marijuana and cocaine.. Something went wrong with the deal and he was shot in the street at point blank range. He felt terrible about going to buy the drugs. He told me that he felt he had been stupid to make such a poor choice. He said that he could not get over what he had done to his parents, now that he could see how much they were suffering. He wanted to talk with his dad to tell him all the things he was telling me. Sadly he never got that opportunity and I explained to Walter that I had tried but that was all I could do. He would have to accept that his father was not open or ready to hear from him at this time. As Walter sat in a chair in my living room, with his head hanging down resting in his hands and his elbows resting on his thighs, his grandmother appeared standing behind him and the chair. She came to take him over to the spirit side although he had not wanted to go. So, I talked to Walter for awhile and let him know he would be ok, his parents would be ok, and that he needed to go with his grandmother. I explained that she would take him home and he would be able to come back and visit if he wanted to see his parents and that she would show him how to do that. After some coaxing, he did go into the light as we say, and home with his grandmother. I never saw Walter or William again.

The encounter affected me so profoundly that it eventually led me to make a commitment to the spirit world that I would be determined to keep. Just as I had given up on my spirit friends, determined to live by the rules that most people live by, the spirit world spoke to me loud and clear, in a very unforgettable way. They proved to me, in no uncertain terms, that this other world that I had come to know was not just in my imagination – that I was not crazy – and that it was all real…very real. So I told the spirit world from that point forward, that I would give them one day a week of my life, to serve them and do their work. I did and I started scheduling that one day for readings, which eventually led to two days, and as word spread then three and so on.

It eventually became difficult to maintain my businesses and keep up with the increasing demands of my work with the spirit world. I found myself working all day and then coming home to do readings by phone until late at night. I was becoming exhausted and equally dissatisfied with my work at the spa and the gym. So, I eventually made the decision to sell the spa and devote all of my time to helping others by giving readings and teaching classes.

Chapter 9
Fear of Spiders

Fear of Spiders

Throughout my life, there have been very few things I have been afraid of, I don't know how or when my fear of spiders began. As long as I can remember I have always been afraid of them. I know that it is irrational and quite silly, after all there are so many more dangerous things in this world to fear. I have done my best to deal with my fear of spiders by being rational and keeping my emotions under control. I can do pretty well most of the time, but certainly some of the larger varieties, with hairy legs, and especially the ones here in Florida, will send me running and screaming out of the room in hysterics. What can I say? We all have our issues,

I have tried to trace back to the moment I first became afraid of them, but have not been able to pinpoint a single incident. While other people have nightmares about being chased by a faceless man, or ghosts and imaginary monsters, I have nightmares about spiders. I don't have them often but they have been a reoccurring theme in my dreams throughout my entire life, What I have come to recognize is that in my dreams, spiders are a symbol which represents all sorts of other fears. I also find it ironic that I have been bitten four separate times by spiders over the years and got actually quite sick from one of them. I am surprised that I have not yet woken with an uncontrollable urge to scale tall buildings in tights and chase bad guys, while I swing from skyscraper to skyscraper on my web!

I still remember many of the spider nightmares vividly. As I stated before, in my younger years, they often took place back in the bathroom in my attic. As I grew older, the spiders in my dreams got bigger, resembling more of the tarantula variety. I would encounter them in all sorts of different places, In my dreams, they would fall on me from the ceiling, or I would get stuck in their webs. I was even backed into a corner by a giant mutant version. I also came to realize that the dreams always occurred at times in my life where I felt very afraid for some reason and often in a situation where I was feeling trapped, They usually occurred during times in my life when I was struggling with fears revolving around my self expression. One of the most difficult struggles I have had in this life is finding the courage to just be who I am – authentically – and publicly. I have always been afraid that if I told people about my abilities that they would think I was crazy. I thought they would laugh at me, think I was weird, reject me, or even worse, accuse me of being a fraud. I was quite certain, at the very least, that they would not believe me.

    I came to realize that because my father had been institutionalized most of his adult life for hearing voices and being "schizophrenic," I grew up being afraid of him. Even worse, I was afraid I was like him. The fear of being hospitalized, like he had been, stayed with me for many years,

    To make matters worse, my mother's extreme religious beliefs meant not only was she not at *all* open to this sort of thing, she was totally condemning of it. My grandmother, on my father's side, was the same way and they both believed that all contact from the spirit world was actually Satan in disguise, who was out to trick us into stealing our souls, by leading us down the wrong path. Talk about overcoming some obstacles – I had my work cut out for me.

    I spent my early life doing my best to appear normal – terrified to ever let anyone see the real me. At one confusing time during my divorce in my early thirties, I even questioned if the experiences that I had were real, wondering if I might, in fact be "crazy", like I had been told my father was. I have spent my entire life contemplating the boundaries between being a medium and a schizophrenic. Where did one end and the other begin? How many other people in mental institutions were diagnosed as mentally ill when, in fact, they were really seeing and hearing spirits just as I did? I am certain there are many adults and children who have been hospitalized and put on prescription medications to control their "hallucinations," when in fact a portion of them may not be delusional at all. This "gift" was a lot to deal with as a young girl. It carried with it much responsibility and until very recently in my life, it felt much more like a curse than a blessing.

    So, I have come to the conclusion that my unconscious mind and the spirit world found a simple way to awaken me to my fears by disguising them as spiders. My fear of spiders has become a symbolism that the spirit world some times uses to alert me to danger, while other times, to encourage me to have the courage to face my fears.

As I mentioned, many times the dreams were quite frequent and intense, especially around the time of my divorce when I began to really question myself and the false persona I was presenting to the world. During this time I decided to stop trying to appear "normal" and just be who I was, risking others approval or not. I felt quite alone at this point in my life and with little to no support. It was during this turning point in my life that I began to confront my fears of rejection, disapproval, ridicule and being alone and shortly after my divorce and my experience with Walter, I had one of the most memorable spider dreams that I have ever had.

I was walking alone, across a vast desert. The ground had been muddy but had dried out and was now hard under my feet. It had millions of cracks running in every direction. As I walked, I noticed that there were literally thousands of tarantulas as far as I could see, all over the ground. They were lying on their backs with their legs curled up. I realized in that moment, they were all dead so I was not afraid. I also realized what the dream represented – that I had finally faced down my most terrifying fears and put them to rest once and for all. I was finally free –free to be me,

Although I still do not like spiders, I don't think I am as terrified as I once was. I will avoid them as much as possible, and definitely would not want to touch one, but I am not as hysterical when I come across them. I have also overcome all of the fears that the spiders once represented to me in those dreams. I have no fear any longer of what people will think of me or what I do. Sure plenty of people don't believe and I know that many believe I am crazy or simply a fraud. That's ok with me now, because I finally know who I am, what I came here to do and have proven to myself that I am not crazy. Once we know something about ourselves, when we really finally know who we are, we no longer give our personal power away to those who like to bring us down. To this day, every time I run into a large spider, which is actually quite often where I live, I am grateful for another opportunity to test myself and confront my fears. In doing so, I become more and more confident in who I am and the power that I hold within myself to overcome all of life's challenges. As is the case with most of our fears, what we imagine is usually much more frightening than the actual reality of the danger we face in a given situation.

Although my spiders are now dead so to speak, I still face plenty of challenging people in my work who sometimes may have a difficult time believing in and understanding what I do. In some cases, I have even encountered hostile and threatening people who merely reflect back to me how threatening and scary my work can be to those who have never directly experienced its healing power; and who's strongly held belief systems may be profoundly challenged by its validity. Every one of these people offers me an opportunity to test my self and practice holding my ground in the face of opposition and hostility. The difference now, is that I no longer fear having these encounters, so they no longer have power over me. Just as I was taught while training in the martial arts, I have learned to redirect the hostile energy and to avoid wasting my own energy fighting with resistance. Instead, I sit back in a relaxed state and wait for an opening to appear. If no opening appears, then I don't waste my energy trying to convince people; I just move on and save my energy for another try later. Although, I no longer have a fear about these encounters, they do continue to offer me an opportunity to test my patience and capacity for compassion and forgiveness, which I am always working on.

Once I came to understand that my antagonists and challengers are actually my teachers, whose purpose is to test me and my fears, I ceased being a victim and began taking charge of my life. It is a very important lesson for all of us to learn. We are not victims here. We are all volunteers and we choose this life and our experiences. Viewing a sparring match between two martial artists, one would notice that they bow to one another before they begin to fight. We are taught in the martial arts that our competitor, adversary and enemy is our teacher, offering us an opportunity to challenge ourselves to reach higher potentials. The match challenges us to face our competitor strategically, but without resistance. We are not there as victims, we are volunteers. We bow to our competitor out of respect, honor and gratitude for their willingness to participate with us in our mutual learning. It is just the same with the people in our lives. Those we come to see as adversaries are really our teachers, and we must honor them and be grateful for their participation in our lives and the lessons they teach us. Once we do that, we are no longer stuck in the powerless role of the victim or feel the need to be the victimizer to regain our power and control. Sometimes the people in our lives teach us by showing us the right way to do things, and sometimes they teach us by showing us the wrong way to do things.

the messenger

Pete Sampras often credited Andre Agassi for his greatness as a tennis champion because he repeatedly challenged him to become a better and better competitor. When we view the people and events in our lives this way, our lives take on a whole new meaning. We are all here to challenge and support one another to overcome and rise above so that we may become our best selves. We are all here and in each others lives to teach and to learn from one another.

There are so many spirits that I have met over the years that have touched my life, inspired me and taught me important lessons. I could never mention all of them, however, the next story is about a spirit that I met who helped me to really understand this very important principle that operates in all of our lives here in the physical world.

Chapter 10
The Spirit Side of Life – The Coma

The Spirit Side of Life – The Coma

Over the years I have read for literally thousands of people, families and spirits. It is impossible to remember most of their stories but I must admit there are a few that stand out through time and which I could never possibly forget. The story of Nathan and Cindy is one of those stories. Just as the valuable new insight that we are not victims here; we are volunteers, was beginning to really permeate my consciousness, I read for Cindy. And, through Nathan, I really understood what this principle was all about.

It was a balmy, hot and humid late spring day and my schedule was very light with only two readings by telephone. The first reading went very well with not too much out of the ordinary. It was for an older woman who wanted to connect with her family. I was all warmed up and ready to go when I picked up the phone to call Cindy – nothing could have prepared me for what would become one of the most profound, enlightening and impressive readings of my life.

When my Office Assistant Lee books my readings, I have asked her to not reveal any details she may know to me about the person prior to the reading. I like to read with no prior knowledge so that my mind is clear and my intuition is unencumbered by memories of past readings or anything the client has told Lee in booking the appointment. When I read for a person a second time around, I typically will not remember much of a prior reading, if anything at all. So, when I picked up the phone for Cindy I had no idea that I had read for her before and her name did not sound familiar to me. Her boyfriend had given her a gift certificate for Christmas the year before, so at that time, she only scheduled with her first name.

The reading began in the usual fashion and she was very friendly and open. I asked if I had read for her before and she answered that I had about a year and a half earlier. The first spirit that came to me was that of a girl who was young at the time of her death. I estimated her to be around seven or eight when she passed. She told me she died in a car accident and that Cindy was her mother. I gave this to Cindy and asked for validation, which she immediately confirmed. Her daughter began to show me the scene of the accident and as she did, I began to have a vague recollection of seeing this scene before. She and her mother were going through an intersection with the green light, when a car ran the red light and plowed straight into the passenger side where her daughter was seated, killing her almost instantly. Cindy was fortunate or perhaps unfortunate enough to have survived the accident. I relayed several messages to her from her daughter and also her mother. Cindy began to sob softly. Her daughter then told me she was with her daddy and then I saw him appear standing next to her holding her hand.

Nathan, the little girls Dad, appeared to me to be in his early 40's when he died. He proceeded to tell me that he was addicted to prescription pain pills and had accidentally overdosed on them which had resulted in a brain aneurism. As I relayed this to Cindy and waited for her feedback and validation, there was a pause and a moment of silence.

"Cindy, are you there? Is this correct, is her father's name Nathan?"

Cindy was speechless and could barely get the words out of her mouth, "Yes, her father is Nathan. He did overdose on pills, but he is not dead. He is in a coma right now as we speak and has been for the past three days."

I was little a surprised as I had assumed he was dead since I saw him on the spirit side and he was speaking to me. But I had had similar experiences in prior readings with Alzheimer's patients. I have found it is not uncommon for people who are "mentally out of it" with advanced stages of Alzheimer's, dementia, brain cancer, a stroke or sometimes even patients in drug induced unresponsive states, to literally step out of their bodies. This is something that we all commonly do when sleeping and dreaming as well. As long as the body is alive, even if sustained by life support, we cannot completely separate from it. We can however, go out of our bodies and move around in spirit form and we often do. So when we say a loved one with Alzheimer's for example is "really out of it" they quite literally are out of their body many times and are actually beginning their transition to the spirit side of life by going back and forth for a time. We remain tethered to our bodies by a cord of light that is severed only with the death of the physical body, at which time we are then released from this life and able to fully move on to life on the spirit side.

What really did surprise me, however, was the message that Nathan proceeded to bring through in Cindy's reading. Cindy explained to me that she and Nathan had divorced shortly after the death of their daughter, which sadly is often the case for couples who suffer the loss of a child. She also went on to tell me that when I had read for her the year before, her then ex-husband, had listened to the whole reading silently on the other phone in the house. She said she never told me, as her husband was skeptical and just wanted to listen.

Nathan was a very good communicator. He was one of those spirits that preferred to speak to me and his words were exceptionally clear. I could quite literally "hear" him as clearly as I could hear Cindy. He proceeded to tell me in detail about everything that was wrong with his body. He described in great detail which portion of the brain had been damaged, right down to which side of the frontal lobe. He also went on to tell me that the particular part of the brain that was damaged was going to affect his speech and ability to communicate, as well as the motor function of one side of his body. Cindy confirmed to me that everything he said was exactly what the doctors had explained. He told me the damage came from a brain aneurism caused by the pain pills that he overdosed on. He also went on to share some personal messages to further prove that it was really him. He showed me his collection of baseball cards and memorabilia and talked about his love of classic muscle cars and his favorite rock band that they had seen together in concert when they were dating. He gave some very personal messages of apology to Cindy as he believed the failure of their marriage was his fault. Once he had given ample proof that it was really him, he went on to deliver the real message, which would profoundly impact me forever.

Cindy asked him if he was going to live and this is what he said.

"I'm not sure yet, I haven't decided. This was not part of my plan. I really messed up by taking those pills…the addiction, this wasn't supposed to happen. I don't want to come back, I want to stay here with Kristina (their daughter) but they are telling me I have to come back, that I'm not finished yet. They say I have more work to do. I don't want to come back though."

He went on to talk a little about his mom and dad staying with him at his bedside in the hospital and how distraught everyone was. He was especially concerned for his mother and full of remorse and guilt for her pain and anguish. He spoke of feeling very badly about the addiction, not getting help after his family had tried many times in vain to convince him to get help. He expressed feeling terrible about his situation and the pain it was causing his family. He asked Cindy to deliver a message to his mom. He said that whether he lived or died, to wait a few months from now and play this recording for his mom. He knew that even if he lived that he would not be able to tell her himself because of the brain damage effecting his speech.

"Tell my mom not to be sad… that I don't want her to be sad. Tell her that whether I live or die, whether I come back into my body or not– that it is 'my choice.' If I come back into my body I don't want her to be sad that I am in the state that I'm in because I know exactly what will be wrong with my body. I know everything, and if I come back into my body, it is because I choose too. Please tell her it's all my choice."

He went on to tell us that he knew if he lived he would not be able to speak for awhile. Like a stroke patient he would have to relearn some things all over again. Because he would not be able to speak or in the event he chose not to come back, he wanted his mother to hear his message.

A few years earlier I had also done another reading that had a similar theme and also made quite an impact on me. I was doing a reading for a group of ten people at a local yoga studio. There was a woman in the group whom I estimated to be in her mid-sixties. I connected with her husband, who had been passed for quite a while – ten years or more. At the time of the reading, she had a son who was forty-two and was living in a nursing care facility. He had been institutionalized all of his adult life. Her husband began to speak to her about her son who we had not discussed to this point.

"Do you have a son who is a paraplegic?" I asked her. She nodded, as her eyes widened. "Your husband would like to talk about him a little. He is telling me that you have suffered for many years over the guilt you feel for having your son in a nursing home."

With that she became very emotional, and began to rummage around in her purse for a tissue.

"He is telling me that your son was in a motorcycle accident when he was about twenty-two I think, is that right?" She nods yes and I take a moment to tune into her sons energy before proceeding.

the messenger

"Your son feels like a child to me, his mind is like a child's. Is that correct?" I ask her.

She tells me yes and explains how the accident paralyzed him from the neck down and caused brain damage and that his brain is like that of an eight or ten year old child.

"Your husband wants to explain something to you. He wants you to understand a few things about your son. He does not want you to feel guilty anymore about having him cared for in a nursing home." The husband shows me a picture of her son in a wheelchair, with a brace connected to the chair behind his neck, supporting his head. This makes me aware that he cannot even move or hold his head upright. He also has no use of his hands or legs. I describe to her the picture that her husband is showing me and she nods to me.

"Your husband is telling me, and it is also obvious to me, that there is no way you could care for your son, that he needs to be where he is. He says again, that you should not feel guilty about having to put your son in the nursing home."

I proceed to explain some things before I deliver the rest of his message, "I don't know what your beliefs are about life after death," I say to her, "but I can tell you, from the work that I do, I have no doubt in my mind that we reincarnate over and over hundreds maybe thousands of lifetimes." She looks at me intently, listening receptively, with no expression in response to what I'm saying. I don't feel that she is skeptical and I feel certain that she is a believer and knows that I am speaking with her husband. She is open, so I proceed.

"We come here to learn, this is school." I continue, "This is like a metaphorical four years away at college – where your husband is – is home and this is a school. Everything in life is our choice, we are not victims here; we are volunteers. We tend to go around and around with the same primary groups of souls over and over. We often change the relationships we are in with one another as we learn something different in the role of mother than we do child or spouse etc. We choose our parents, where we will be born and live, we even choose when and how we will die."

The whole group is listening to me intently now, as enthralled by my explanation as they had been with this woman's reading.

"Some of us pick one particular exit point and some of us pick two or three possible exit points along our path depending on how our life plan is going. Do you understand?" I ask her and nod. Silently, she nods yes back.

"Okay then, your husband wants you to understand something from that perspective ok? He is telling me that for the past several lifetimes your son has always been a doctor. He chose to work with people who have been physically crippled. He is telling me, in past lifetimes that he has worked with patients who had Polio, Rickets and other physical limitations. He is telling me that your son chose this experience as a paraplegic to learn more about his work, his patients and how it feels from the inside out to be a paraplegic. He chose this experience so that in his next life time he will be a better doctor. He will know more about the body's limitations from the inside and most importantly, it is also an exercise and lesson for him in compassion, so that he may better serve his patients in the next life."

Her eyes are very wide now and tears are streaming down her face but she is smiling. I can see the relief in her face and the surprise as she had never thought about his condition from this perspective, having always seen him as a victim.

"Do you understand he is not a victim? You do not need to feel guilty; he volunteered for this experience to learn and grow and in his great compassion, he chose this so that he could better help others. Your husband also wants you to know that he is okay and that he is not suffering or unhappy. He says that it is a blessing that his mind is like that of a child as he is not really aware of his circumstance. He also has no memory of life before the accident and he is also not really able to process the passage of time from one of your visits to the next." She nods to me in agreement again.

The husband and her parents also came through with lots of personal details for her, just to make sure that she "knew" this was really them and that it was all real – so that she would be able to believe the messages about her son that she so desperately needed to hear.

All of those little details in the readings, the nicknames, manner of death, details of diseases, childhood memories – they are all to "provide proof." They give proof that this is real, that I am real, and most importantly, that I am actually doing what I claim to be doing – speaking to their loved ones on the spirit side. All of these things are details that I could never know – could not possibly guess – things that only my client and their loved one would know. The proof is always in the details. Once I have proven to the person I am reading for that it is really their loved one, then they are open and able to believe the real messages that the spirit world wants to bring through. In both of these cases the message was that we are not

the messenger

victims here in life, no matter how things appear. We are all volunteers. Nothing about our lives is random or unplanned and *everything happens for a reason* and a greater purpose.

I learned early on doing this work, that it was essential to bring through evidential details that I would have had no possible way of knowing. It was the only way I could get a person's attention and them to believe without question, allowing them to be open to receiving the messages the spirit world needed to get through to them. Sometimes skeptical people think that I'm not really speaking to the dead, but instead that I am a psychic mind-reader – a telepath. Spirit has a great way of curing that skepticism by bringing through things that the person I'm reading for does not even know at the time of the reading. For example, they might tell me that their mom had given up a baby for adoption when she was seventeen and my client never knew. I always instruct the client to ask other family members and when they invariably validate the message it is a very profound and often life altering experience for them. Spirits will also often bring through messages or signs that will come to pass in the future as another way to remedy those that think I'm a mind reader or have some how gotten their personal information.

I will never forget when I did a reading for a lady dentist in a group once, and the whole reading was about the television show *American Idol*, the season when Taylor Hicks was a contestant. I described to her in great detail scenes from New York City, sitting at the show in the front row of the audience and even going back stage meeting Taylor Hicks. She had no idea what I was talking about and in a very annoyed tone informed me that she didn't really even like the show and had only watched it once. I'm pretty sure she left that night thinking I was full of it and was disappointed and I must admit I was left a little puzzled myself. That is until four weeks later when she called me to book a private reading. She practically exploded with excitement in my office as she proceeded to tell me that three weeks after the group reading, her mother won tickets on the radio to see *American Idol* and they flew her mom and her to New York City, where they sat in the front row and went backstage and hung out with Taylor Hicks! It's one of my favorite stories to tell to this day.

Chapter 11
"Break on Through to the Other Side"

—Jim Morrison

"Break on Through to the Other Side"
— Jim Morrison

I have developed over the years, a certain level of detachment from the work that I do, and the people that I work with. It is a necessary survival tool, much like the detachment developed by a police officer, social worker or therapist. When one is constantly faced with the tragedy and trauma of life and death situations day after day, it is the only way you can maintain a separation between where others end and you begin. For me in my work, in addition to "seeing" tragic events like suicide, homicide and accidents, I have the additional burden of reliving them and actually feeling them to some extent. When I relive with a mother how she found her three-year-old in the bottom of the swimming pool in their backyard for example, I am quite literally feeling the pain and anguish of the mother. Being a mom myself, it can sometimes be difficult to maintain my own composure and let the feelings and experience go at the end of the day. As another example, in trying to help a man's widow understand why he would take his own life, and I am describing the pain and suffering he went through just before he made the fatal decision, I am feeling not only his emotions but hers as well. It can be very draining and many times very difficult for me. I have developed a thick skin through the years and that mental and emotional detachment serves me well in the face of such human suffering. I also know that my work is for the purpose of healing and that within the greatest tragedy and human suffering is also a message of love and hope that serves to always remind me why I relive such horrific experiences for those I am here to help. The messages change people's lives and give them the peace and closure that they need in order to move on with their own life. The constant reminder that we are not alone – that everything happens for a reason and that life is about learning and Love – is what sustains me.

Due to the fact that I am always dealing with strangers whose lives have no personal connection to my own, that detachment has served me well and has been easy to maintain. I do not become emotionally involved once the reading is over because I do not typically know the people or the spirits that I am working with. However, that would all change the summer of 2008 when my work world would suddenly and violently collide with my own life in a very personal and sentimental way…

The air was thick and heavy and the dampness saturated my skin and clothing within minutes of walking outside. The first week of August in Key West is like living in a steam room. It's peak hurricane season, there is plenty of rain and the humidity is close to one hundred percent. As I opened the car door and sat down in the driver's seat, it was as if I was opening an oven door and a thick wave of heat washed over me. I kept the doors open and let the air-conditioning run a few minutes while I waited for the steering wheel to cool down enough that I could actually grip it without burning my hands.

I've been in Key West now for sixteen years; it's hard to believe it's been that long since I left Baltimore. I tried to keep in touch with a few friends for the first few years after I'd left, but it was difficult being so young and so far away from home. My social life in Key West as a young single woman was busy and exciting, so I really did not think to often of home or the friends that I'd left behind. I began to get lost in the years and time passed by, as eventually marriage, motherhood and owning two businesses quickly consumed my life. I made lots of new friends in Key West and after just a few years I had lost touch with most of my friends in Baltimore. I refer to Key West as "Never Neverland" because it has a way of sucking you into its alternate reality and time seems to just stand still. Isolated from the real world and far away from the hustle and bustle of mainland life, one day you look up to realize that sixteen years has gone by. I had never really stopped to think about it much but, this day would be the day I would receive my wake-up call. It was the day that would set loose a sequence of events that would remind me just how long I had been away.

I've been really tired all week, kind of drained for some reason. It happens

the messenger

from time to time when I am busy doing a lot of readings. Connecting with spirits all week long can cause quite an energy drain, especially on the weeks I work with the sudden death & suicide groups. Although I have learned to manage my energy pretty well and have come to recognize when I need a break, this week has not been particularly busy or taxing so I am not sure why I am feeling so tired. I was also quite frustrated this morning with my computer acting up and could not check my emails. All week long the computer has been randomly shutting off, right in the middle of what ever I am doing, for no apparent reason, and then coming back on again several minutes later by itself. I have lost my work a few times in the process and had spent the morning answering emails only to lose one just after I had finished typing a lengthy reply to an inquiry about a haunting. The computer is less than a year old and should not be having these problems. I ran the virus scan, no viruses, so I figure it must be some hardware problem and I've already decided after I'm done with work today to run it up to the Geek Squad for repair.

It is important to note, that just as I had previously been with Walter, I had been feeling listless and just not right for the past few days and had also been experiencing computer problems.

As the air-conditioning begins to get cold and the car finally cools down, I close the door putting it in reverse and begin to back out of the driveway. My cell phone rings and I stop the car and look at the caller ID. It's a Baltimore area code but no number that I recognize. Perhaps it's a client.

"Hello?"

"Hi, is this Denise?" a man's voice says, sounding a little apprehensive. I do not recognize the voice.

"Yes, this is."

"Denise this is Steve....Steve Lynch...from high school," with the tone in his voice sounding more like a question than a statement.

I reply, stunned and very surprised, "Oh my God, Steve! Hi! How are you? WOW, I haven't talked to you in like twenty-five years I think? Probably, since about tenth grade...right?"

Laughing a little nervously, but also happy and cheerful that I obviously remembered him, he says, "Yeah, at least that long I think."

Steve didn't actually go to Towson High; he went to Boys Latin one of the prep schools in the area. He lived near my best friend Lindsey, and I mainly knew him through her. He had been a good friend of her boyfriend, Will. Lindsey was two years older than me, so when I was a junior, she went off to college. Although she and I stayed in touch, I never really saw Steve after that – not since I was about sixteen. Steve was kind of a nerdy kid, sort of awkward but funny at the same time.

"How did you find me Steve? How did you get my number? I didn't think anyone knew where I was or how to find me with my married name?"

"Well, I found Lindsey by calling one of our old friends from school, John, who knew she was in Virginia and her married name and I figured she would know how to get a hold of you. I'm not sure if you heard or not about Nick, but I figured since you dated Julian for so long you would want to know. I remember that you were really close to his family. He was killed last week in a car accident and the services were yesterday."

"What! Oh my God, no I had no idea! What happened?" I asked, stunned.

"Well, my wife worked with him and she grew up with him and Julian and went to Dumbarton Middle School with them. He was driving home from work and lost control of the car and ran off the side of the road. He lived out in the country by Reisterstown. He was married and had two little kids."

"Oh my God, Steve that is just terrible!" I was shocked, not only by the news but also the call from Steve. "I can't believe it... Who is your wife? Do I know her?" I queried.

"No, I don't think so. She is about five years younger than us, but she remembers you. I know it is kind of weird that I'd call you after all these years, but I don't know why...I just thought you would want to know."

"No, Steve it's fine... really. Thank you so much for calling me, for even thinking to call me. You know I have not really kept in touch with anyone but Lindsey, so I probably would have never found out. Yeah, I really appreciate the call."

We stayed on the phone for about fifteen minutes just catching up on each other's lives and what we had been doing since high school. He was married with four kids and he filled me in on what some of our old friends were doing now. It was a nice conversation and we laughed about some old memories of our teenage exploits and both agreed that we hoped our own children were much better behaved than we had been. So far they were, thankfully.

I hung up the phone and just sat in the car for a few minutes trying to process the news that had instantly transported me back in time twenty-five years ago. During our conversation, he recalled memories of our teen years that I had completely forgotten until he reminded me. In fact, I never

the messenger

have really spent much time thinking about the past. I'm more of a person who is always looking forward and spend much more time thinking about and visualizing the future then reminiscing about the past. That was until now. Driving to my office, my mind was flooded with memories of long forgotten places and people, memories that I had not thought about for a very, very long time.

After dinner I was busy on the computer searching for newspaper articles, an obituary or anything that would give me more information about Nick, his family and the details of the accident. Steve did not know much about it or any of the details. He also didn't know much about Julian or their mom either when I had asked if he knew where Julian was. He had told me that all he knew was that Julian was living in LA and that he was at the funeral and that he had stayed by his mom's side the whole time. He did tell me there must have been five hundred people at the funeral, which did not surprise me because the Nick I had known always had a lot of friends.

It had only been six days since his death and I began to put two and two together. Why hadn't I realized it before – my energy feeling so drained, the vague feeling of sadness and depression that had been lingering with me all week for no reason and the problems with the computer? Memories of Walter and William began flashing in my mind, and then I realized it must be Nick. He must have been hanging around the house the last few days - the same as when Walter had died. I remember that it took me almost a week then to realize what was happening.

I have learned a lot since my encounter with Walter. It is different when a person in spirit is still here on the earth plane. Contrary to what one might think, it is actually more difficult for me to pick them up in an earthbound state then once they have crossed over into the spirit side of life. I would estimate that about ninety-five percent of all the spirits that I connect with in readings have already crossed over. Only maybe five percent are still here on the earth plane.

When I first started working with the support groups, I found it difficult sometimes to connect with spirits that had died of a drug overdose or by suicide. I eventually figured out that the reason is, that sometimes the person will stay here on the earth plane for awhile before crossing over and while they are still here their energy is on a much lower frequency than the people who have crossed over to the spirit side. I have had to learn to "tune" my receiver into a different frequency of energy in order to connect with them. That is the best way that I can describe it.

Imagine for a moment if you will, that I am like a very sensitive radio receiver. Most receivers (people) can tune into the frequencies 92.0 and 107.5 on the radio dial. These are the frequencies of energy that the physical senses perceive through sight, sound and touch. I on the other hand, can not only tune into those frequencies, but can also pick up those frequencies below and above – like down to 68.5 and up to 149.5. For most readings with people who are on the spirit side, I tune into frequencies around the 140's, but for an earthbound spirit, their frequency is around the 70's metaphorically speaking. And, it will stay low until they cross over. Then their frequency will rise up as they grow in understanding and begin healing and return to their original spiritual state.

Life on the spirit side exists on frequencies of energy that are much higher and faster than those here in the physical world. There are also colors and sounds there that we do not see or hear here. So, if I'm walking around with my receiver set on 143.0 I can totally miss someone coming through on 72.5. I have to actually stop and change the dial and adjust my receiver to the lower frequency to tune them in clearly. It is also important to remember that connecting with spirits is my job and just like most people, when I'm off work I want to spend time with my family, doing normal everyday stuff – not talking to spirits. I have also become very good at tuning out the sprit world when I'm not working. I realized early on it was important to establish some boundaries with those on the spirit side, so that I could maintain some semblance of a normal life. Just like a doctor would not like his patients calling and knocking on the door of his home at all hours, neither do I. And just as a doctor would, I prefer to work by appointment. However, there are still some occasions where the spirit world is bound and determined to break on through and get my attention and this was clearly one of those occasions.

I could not help but think about how totally random and out of the blue it was for Steve to even think about getting in touch with me after twenty-five years as we had not really been close. However, I know nothing is really ever random here on earth, and I also know that spirits are very good at impressing thoughts upon our minds. I was sure that was exactly what Nick had done. Knowing my past connection with Steve, he had impressed Steve with the thought to call me. I found the obituary online, which mentioned Nick's surviving relatives including Julian and Nick's mom Ann. I have wondered about her from time to time over the years as I was very close to her when I was dating Julian.

the messenger

My relationship with my own mom has always been difficult. She was only twenty-one when I was born and she divorced my dad when I was just a few years old. As a single mom, she worked full-time to support us, which left me on my own a lot of the time. My young life was what I like to refer to as "spiritual boot camp." During those years, I was exposed to a motherload of information about theology, religion and man's concepts regarding life after death and God. For the few years my mom was married to my dad, she was an enthusiastic and dutiful member of the Kingdom Hall of Jehovah's Witnesses. She was recruited into the church by my dad's mom. During that time, we did not celebrate Christmas or birthdays and spent Saturday's knocking on doors handing out The *Watchtower* magazine. We were on a mission for God, to find all the lost souls of the world who did not know Jehovah. We had hopes of saving them before the end of the world arrived, which by their calculations, was any day now. At the very wise age of four, I remember vividly, having a conversation with my grandmother, expressing that I did not want to go to the Kingdom Hall anymore. I did not like it there and I especially did not like the man who preached to us. My grandmother, who insisted I must go, was quite astonished when I proclaimed that I would not go to a church where they believed that Mother Theresa would not go to heaven. You see, the Jehovah's Witnesses believe they are the only ones that will be let into the Kingdom of God and Mother Theresa, being a Catholic, would not qualify for entry, even though she spent her entire life selflessly in service to others. Somehow at this very young age, I had understood what a wonderful woman Mother Theresa was and I exclaimed that if she were not allowed into Heaven then I did not want to go either! So began my reputation as a very precocious young girl.

Shortly after my mom divorced my dad, we moved to be near my other grandparents in Baltimore and we converted to the Methodist Church where my mom's mom belonged. I absolutely adored my grandparents and we lived with them until I was about nine. My grandmother had been a life-long Methodist and taught Sunday School at the church and I began going with her. I have fond memories of Sunday School and the Methodist Church. It was a fun and uplifting place to be – full of happy people, totally different than the judgmental Dooms-Day church members I had known at the Kingdom Hall.

When Mom and I moved out on our own around my second grade year, she decided we were no longer going to go to church. She thought that I should be able to make up my own mind about God and religion when I was older. That was fine with me and I was actually quite relieved by her new, freer, stance.

I was a "latch key kid" as they called it back then. I would get home from school and pretty much take care of myself, until my mom got home from her job at a retail clothing store in the evening. I did not have a particularly stable home life with my mom. I believe that she did the best she could, however, she was pretty consumed with her own life most of the time. She also, unfortunately, had a penchant for drinking too much and was not a particularly nice person when she drank. My unplanned existence, which caused the unwanted marriage to my father, seemed to generate intense feelings in my mom, of shame, resentment and anger towards me. In fact, I have spent much of my lifetime working to overcome that fact. In my young life I was taught at home that love was expressed through control, criticism and anger. Although my childhood was difficult, it taught me to be independent, resourceful and self-reliant. I was also very fortunate to have a very loving extended family that was always there to provide the support I needed when it was sometimes lacking at home. The School of hard knocks as they say, eventually taught me to develop a thick skin in order to protect all of my sensitivity, as well as, a very strong and independent sense of self. These skills have served me well throughout my life and I believe have in many ways, have empowered me and prepared me for the work that I do now.

After my Mom remarried and my brother and sister were born, to her credit, she became determined to create more of a family-like atmosphere. She eventually quit drinking altogether and we then went back to church again, only this time, it was Catholic because Francis, an Italian man, had been raised that way. My mom even went so far as to insist that I be baptized Catholic since she was having my brother baptized too and I had never been. I went to CCD (school to learn Catholic Christian Doctrine) to learn all about what Catholics believe and I begrudgingly got up every Sunday morning to go to the Folk Music Mass, which featured young hip sounding rock music, in an attempt to attract young families into the church. I have mixed feelings and memories about the Catholic Church. On one hand, I loved the big, old historic Baltimore Cathedral; it was so beautiful inside and the energy there from years of people praying felt very spiritual to me. For that reason, to this day I still love to visit old Catholic cathedrals. I also liked all the rituals and chants, although I really could not understand the point of doing them. I also could not help but notice that most everyone in the Mass was just going through the motions and mindlessly repeating the prayers that they had memorized when they were children. It all seemed robotic to me and I questioned if anyone was really even paying attention to the mass or the Priest. As a teenager, I found the church's ideas about life after death and their concept of God and Heaven and Hell to be primitive and full of contradictions. For one, I could not understand how God could be all forgiving and loving and then at the same time send you straight to Hell for eternity if you broke the rules. Then, there were – the rules. I found them way to restrictive and also noticed that practically no one followed them, yet everyone pretended too. So, what was the point of it all really? Incidentally, I fainted in the church a few times. I think it was all the kneeling and standing and kneeling again coupled with the fact that it was always so hot in there. Shortly after my sister was born, Mom and Francis moved about an hour into the country where they began their eventual journey into the newly emerging and rapidly growing Evangelical movement of the nineteen-nineties. For some reason, they decided that they did not agree with the Catholic's worship of the Virgin Mary and that the churches practice of Idolatry with all the saints and statues they prayed too was akin to pagan practices.

It was about this time I drew the proverbial line in the sand and said "that's it...I'm done!" I stopped going to church and at sixteen-years-old, I was old enough and rebellious enough that no one was going to make me go. I do believe that a church community can be an important source of comfort and support for many people. I believe that a church should be a tool for spiritual growth and understanding and a refuge for our soul. I have always understood Jesus' life to have been about living and teaching the principles of unconditional love, forgiveness and compassion. Unfortunately, many times too much of organized religion seems to be more interested in pushing an agenda of power and politics or controlling and recruiting more people, than helping them grow spiritually. Many religious organizations, in my opinion, do not want people who think and feel for themselves and instead want followers. Religious leaders are often taught and teach that people should follow their rules and obey without question. They too often seek to control people by promoting fear - fear of God, fear of death and fear of judgment and damnation. Religion would lose its power and control if people finally realized that they have within them, everything they need to connect with God. It requires only love. Fear of God is an oxymoron as there is only unconditional love, compassion and forgiveness in God's world on the spirit side of life. Fear and judgment are conditions that only exist here in this world. The only judgment we face after death is our own. On the spirit side, the forgiveness we seek does not come from God, but from ourselves and from those we may have harmed intentionally or unintentionally in life. We forgive one another once on the spirit side because we have compassion for one another's human trials and suffering. We have compassion for one another because on the spirit side there is only love and love is the flower that produces the fragrance which is compassion.

My Mom, now an evangelical born-again Baptist, follows a strict fundamentalist doctrine. I believe that she is convinced that the whole family will be in Heaven except me and it saddens me as I know it must break her heart. She refuses to discuss with me what I do and the fact that I am a medium. She has been taught, out of ignorance and misunderstanding, that what I do is channeling Satan and that he pretends to be the loved ones of those I read for, in an attempt to steal people's souls and lead them down the wrong path and away from Christ. Because of this black and white thinking, she refuses to discuss the subject with me and we have not been able to find common ground or address the misunderstanding that exists around my work, to this day.

Ironically, just about the time I had received the call with the news about Nick, I had decided to join the Facebook revolution. Facebook was totally new to me and I had not yet discovered the feature to connect with old classmates, when my high school friend Ellie found me and sent me a friend request. It had also been close to twenty-five years since I had been in touch with her and I was very excited that she had found me. The amazing thing about the Facebook phenomenon is that once you connect with one old friend you begin finding all of your other old friends or they find you.

So, over the next six months I managed to reconnect with my high school graduating class and all of my closest childhood friends. We spent a lot of time catching up with each other through email. We looked at each other's family pictures which were posted online in photo albums and caught up with all the things we had heard about other friends and what they were doing now. Ellie and I began to talk of meeting up in Baltimore. She was now living in Arizona and I in Florida, but both of us needed to make a trip to see family in the spring, so we began coordinating. We invited a few

the messenger

of our old friends who were on Facebook. Word spread and before we knew it we had about fifty people, some flying in from out of town and from three different graduating classes, planning to come to the party. And, what began as a one day party, quickly turned into a weekend, three-day event, as more and more people showed interest in attending.

Chapter 12
The Great Mystery

The Great Mystery

As difficult as it is for some people to believe that what I do is real or that life goes on after death and that our loved ones are still around us; it is equally as difficult for me to understand why that is so hard to believe. To me, it is so natural. In every religion we are taught to believe that life continues after death. I am just simply saying that Heaven is not a far away place that is separate from our physical world. It is actually right here – all around us. It just exists on a higher frequency of energy. I try to explain this by telling people that I am much like a dog. Yes, a dog.

Imagine you are sitting on your couch watching TV and your dog is lying there next to you when he jumps up suddenly and runs across the room and begins barking at the door. Because he can hear noises outside the door, he is alerting you that there are people in the street in front of your house. A dog's ears are much more sensitive to sounds than ours, and they can hear things that we can't. So, just because we can't hear the sound outside the front door, does not mean that the neighbors are not outside talking. Your dog hears them clearly, in just the same way that I can hear people on the spirit side. I can simply tune into the different frequencies of energy where our loved ones on the spirit side reside.

I am merely saying that we are all still connected, that the illusion of us being separate is just that – an illusion. This illusion has been perpetuated over thousands of years throughout history through fear and misunderstanding, coupled with the never-ending quest for governments, in concert with religion, to control and manipulate the masses.

As for those scientific thinkers among us, Albert Einstein, a well-respected thinker for his theories on Relativity and how energy works, was a master of understanding the natural laws that govern life on earth. He was one of the pioneers who began to understand some of the natural laws that govern the universe and he taught us that energy cannot be destroyed; it simply transforms and changes form. So like water transforms into steam, when the physical body is worn out and breaks down, the soul is released and transforms back into its natural a state of pure energy – one that is on a higher, faster frequency. Our personalities, memories and knowledge continue on because death is absolutely an illusion and not real. The details that spirits bring through in readings are proof that we have memory, consciousness and personality outside of the body and the brain. We are not our brains, or what's in our brains. Our brains are simply the computer operating systems that run our bodies and allow us to function and experience life here in the physical world.

Physical death is merely a transformation, like water turning into steam, to a different state of being. Water vapor is still made of hydrogen and oxygen but its density and volume change and in our case, our frequency of energy and density changes. Quantum Physics has proven that all things in the world are made of molecules of energy, which are always moving even in the heaviest and most dense solid objects. We are just bundles of energy and everything is different compositions of energy. Similar to a hermit crab that has outgrown its shell, and moves on to find a new one, our bodies are just our shell. Much like if we were to visit the Moon, they are like a "space suit" that we put on so that we can experience life here in the physical world.

We are actually not invisible in spirit form either. Our pets, small children and animals are very capable of seeing our loved ones in spirit when they pay us a visit. Have you ever noticed your cat or dog acting very strangely after the passing of a loved one? My dog has often jumped up suddenly and began barking at a corner of the room, where to the human eye, it appears to be empty. One night, I watched my grandfather in spirit, take a "virtual" cat toy and play with my very much alive cat. The cat jumped and chased the toy all over my couch for three or four minutes while I and my grandfather in spirit laughed. To anyone else, it would have appeared my cat had quite literally gone insane chasing around and pouncing on an invisible cat toy. But I could see clearly what my cat was chasing and who was playing with him. Often times when a toddler tells you she is playing

the messenger

with Grandpa and he's passed, she is quite literally playing with Grandpa. It is not her imagination or yours; but it is where we most easily see them – in our imaginations and dreams.

It is equally amazing to me that we spend hours of our days in virtual realities that don't really exist but that our mind has come to accept as part of our physical world and "reality" as we know it. I'm referring to the internet. I love the internet and took to it like a fish to water. I had one of the very first internet and email accounts in the early nineties. The internet is an abstract, virtual reality that to me was very easy to grasp from the beginning. We are all regularly surfing the virtual web and connecting with people and places all day long in it. I have spent thousands of dollars on a website, for example, that I cannot touch, hold or really possess physically. Yet I accept that it is real and so do all the others that connect with it. By the same token, we never even stop to question how we can type up a body of text into an email, type in an "address," press the send button, and literally within only seconds, that email will reach another person's computer on the other side of the globe. We don't even stop to consider how all of that energy travels invisibly through time and space almost instantaneously, and is received with all the words in the correct order by one person and one computer out of billions and in only seconds!

It was only twenty-five years ago we would have found that and the fact that we no longer need to put an envelope into a mailbox – waiting weeks for the same message to be received on the other side of the globe – astonishing.

My fourteen-year-old spends hours a day in the "virtual realities" of dragons, warriors and aliens, battling along with players from all over the world. Why then, is it so difficult for us to accept that the miracle of a life, which is so much more complex than a video game or computer, would not be able to continue beyond the limitations of time, space and the physical body? Are we not already challenging the boundaries of time and space every time we send an email? I'd also like to point out that electricity existed long before we discovered it. Two hundred years ago, it would have been quite miraculous that we would flick a switch on the wall and the lights would come on. We do not question that the electricity that we cannot see, flows from the switch to the bulb. If we could travel back in time a thousand years ago, one might be thought of as a witch or a god just because they could turn a flashlight on.

We are not our bodies we are merely living in them for a short time.

Our physical bodies are neither the end nor the beginning of our life, they are more like the vehicle we use to travel from this life to the other and navigate in while here visiting Earth. Death is not the end of life but merely a part of life and a transition from this life back to our home. Earth life is nothing more than school for us and even a vacation away from our home. It is a metaphorical four years away at college where we come to learn and where we can enjoy all the pleasurable nuances that only physical existence can offer.

People have pondered the Great Mystery of who we are and why we are here since the beginning of time. The spirit world has taught me that we come here to learn and the lessons that we take are contained within our life experiences, within our families and through our relationships. "We choose" our life experiences and circumstances before we are ever born. We choose our families, our culture and even our race. We choose the people and circumstances in our lives so that we (our souls), can learn and grow. We are not victims here in life, we are volunteers. We are not sent here, we choose to come here. When I explain this, people will often ask, "Why would I pick such a terrible or abusive parent?" for example. Well it's simple really. We would pick them because their shortcomings, which are the lessons that they have come here to learn, provide the backdrop or classroom for the lessons that we have come here to learn. I can tell you that I have learned, without a doubt, that absolutely nothing in this life is random or without purpose. Everything really does happen for a reason and to teach us something that we came here to learn, even if we do not understand it during this lifetime.

The love we share, the emotional ties, are the glue that keep us together and working on our lessons. Fate is nothing more than God and our helpers on the spirit side behind the scenes coordinating the timing of events in our lives. The "fuel" that keeps us going and feeds our souls is love. Our life is a stage and we are the actors. We learn different lessons through the roles that we play. Although we arrange our circumstances, lessons, opportunities and challenges in advance, our outcomes are not written. Ultimately we choose our outcomes by the choices that we make in our lives. We come here to learn, grow and make choices and those choices determine our outcomes and the direction our life will take. If we want peace in our lives and on our planet, then we must act out our roles with love - because without love we are running on empty. Without love, life becomes lifeless and we become diseased in our mind, body and spirit.

the messenger

When we are starved of love, we slowly die inside and regress to a survival mode of existence where life is reduced to a "fight or flight - kill or be killed" mentality. The only way to rise above this primitive state of existence is through love. The way to peace is love. The only way to God is through love. Love not only for God, but for ourselves and for one another.

Where we often get stuck on the subject of death and life after death is, humankind wants to debate over who is right and who is wrong. Is it religion or science and which religion and which theory from science has the right answers? Spirit has taught me this, *"that all paths of knowledge, all theories of thought hold a piece of the truth, no one path, or theory, science or religion for that matter, hold's all of the truth. There are true elements on all sides, yet no one path contains all the answers."* We come here to take many different classes and learn many different lessons, but the main lessons that we all come here to learn, one way or another are; unconditional love, compassion and forgiveness. Every message, from every spirit and reading I have ever done, has something to do with one or more of these three elements. Every problem on earth has a solution that lies within one of these three lessons. Humanity, religion & science can all find common ground within love, compassion and forgiveness.

I know this statement will set a lot of people off, however it is the truth. All sources of knowledge, whether religious or scientific in origin, are limited in scope by the many limitations of human existence, experience and understanding. The existence of life and life after death is explained partially by the natural laws that we have come to understand through science, as well as many of the spiritual philosophies created by religion. From my perspective, I would say they both contain elements of the truth, and when put together, show the real picture of who we are, why we are here and where we go when we die.

The problem with all man-made theories is just that, they are man made and based on the limitations of the current knowledge of the times and understanding derived from the past. They are very limited in scope for that reason. The greatest obstacle to real understanding is arrogance and dogma, which are found as equally among the spiritual circles, as they are within the scientific circles. Because of our incessant need to maintain and be in control, most people are more concerned with being right than with what is the truth. I hope that people will begin to realize that science and religion are not opposing forces, but more like left and right hands.

The world will finally know peace when the world's religions begin to realize that they are not in opposition to one another, but merely different disciplines and classrooms that we are studying in here at school. Each one is teaching its own set of lessons; just as we would go to college and choose to take different courses of study. It doesn't mean one is any better than another, they are just different and we need all of them. If we could all begin to open our minds and to respect one another's perspectives and knowledge, we would let go of our need to be right and to be in control. Then we might all begin to realize that together, we present a more complete understanding and image of the bigger picture.

Coming from the deeply Christian background that I have, I feel that I must briefly address the Bible. However, I do so reluctantly, as I realize that this is always a highly charged and divisive subject. I would like only to suggest, that I think it is important to recognize that the Bible was written over two-thousand years ago by men of that time who had a much more limited understanding of the world they lived in than we do today. It was also a time in history when more than ninety-five percent of the population was illiterate.

I want to be very clear, that I am in no way questioning or disputing the historical record or validity of the Bible, or the life of Jesus. I am merely suggesting that I believe it is important to recognize that humankind's understanding has grown and evolved intellectually, scientifically, culturally, and as such, spiritually, in the last two thousand years. To try and hold firm to a strict and literal interpretation of the Bible at this point would be to adopt a very limited and outdated understanding of the spiritual world. It would be much like continuing to insist in this day and age, that the world is flat and if you sail too far into the ocean you will fall off the edge. I believe that the Bible should be kept in context with the understanding of the times in which it was written. In much the same way, a fifth grade math student today would not argue with a second grade math student that their understanding of math is right and the second graders understanding of math is wrong. Instead, we grow to understand that they are in fact both right, but that the fifth grader simply has continued to learn and grow, and as such, has expanded his understanding of the basic math principles beyond what he learned previously. By the same token, one could explain to the second grader, the fifth grade math concepts until they were blue in the face, but the second grader will not understand these concepts himself, until he has completed the lessons of third and fourth grade math. This understanding helps us to have compassion and patience with those who may have a more limited understanding of life on the spirit side.

the messenger

I always spend time in meditation before working with the spirit world – sometimes ten minutes and sometimes thirty minutes. It depends on my state of mind and life at the time, how long it takes me to get into the right vibration or frequency. Because I cannot actually go into the spirit world and up to their frequency, we have to meet in what I like to refer to as a middle place – an in between place – or as my grandfather on the spirit side calls it - "the holding tank."

The holding tank is where spirits meet me and get ready to work with me. My grandfather on the spirit side is my assistant. While I get the people ready and organized on this side of life, he does the same with everyone I will work with on that side. He explains to everyone before we begin how I like to work and how best to work with me, while I explain the same to my clients on this side. In order for me to meet them in the middle space, I have to raise my own vibration, my frequency of energy way up and they have to slow theirs way down and then we can "meet each other in the middle." I would best describe it as if I am standing right at the entrance of the tunnel of white light you hear so often about in Near Death Experiences. Occasionally however, in a reading, some spirits will actually prefer to just come right here and will stand in my office and communicate with me here. We communicate telepathically and they will speak to me with words in thought, show me pictures and images and impress upon me physical and emotional feelings. I am also a medical intuitive, so that means that I can detect and identify disease in the body or a disease someone had in life while they were in the body. I am also a remote viewer, so I can look into other places in the physical world.

I have all the psychic abilities and use them all while connecting with spirits in my readings; Clairvoyance "clear-seeing", Clairaudience "clear-hearing", Clairsentience "clear-feeling or sensing" and Clairambience "clear-smelling." Every spirit also communicates with me differently according to their level of understanding of how the process works and their personal preference and communication style – just as they would have in life. Some quite literally speak to me in conversations, as clear as I would hear a person; while others may show me pictures and symbols and it can be a bit like playing a game of charades! They also will impress me with feelings and information and I will just know things, without really being able to say how I know them – I just do. Because of the difference in energy and vibration between this world and the spirit side, they communicate with me much faster than we do here. Although I can telepathically communicate with them at their same speed, I have to slow down a lot when I deliver the messages to the client. Many times I will sit and listen for a few seconds, absorbing everything the spirits want to tell me and then tell my client much more slowly, just as a translator would do.

When my son was four, he used to wake up all the time in the middle of the night crying. One night I asked him what was wrong, and he told me that he could not sleep because he kept hearing all these people in his room whispering. It also scared him because he could only hear them and couldn't see them. So, when I asked him what they were saying, he answered "I don't know Mom, they talk too fast. I can't understand them." I knew right then that he could hear spirits too. So he began to sleep with his TV on throughout most of his childhood so that the noise would drown out their chatter and he could sleep. He has seen a few spirits in our house from time to time as well. He is a typical teen boy though, and shows very little interest in the whole thing. My family is pretty used to all the activity in our house and my husband and son have witnessed a lot of it first hand. They view it all as just a part of our life and no big deal.

Chapter 13
Virtual Reunions

Virtual Reunions

The obituary I found online named Nick's widow, whom Id never met, and their two children, and said that they were from Reisterstown, Maryland. I was unable to find any newspaper articles about the accident. For the next week Nick was all I could think about and as spirits often do, he had been invading my dreams almost nightly. In fact, it is not at all uncommon for me to read for a group of people in the evening and then come home and go to bed only to wake at two a.m. with the spirits from the evening chattering away to me in my head and my dreams. Most people do not realize how easy it is for the spirits of our loved ones to communicate with us in our dreams.

Our loved ones will often visit us in our dreams, especially those of us who are not trained in connecting with them. It is during sleep, in our dreams, that the rational intellect part of the brain is turned off and on auto pilot, rendering it unable to interfere with our intuitive receptivity and perceptions. Many times when we think we are dreaming of visiting Grandma, Grandma is quite literally, visiting us telepathically. Much like spirits communicate with me telepathically during a reading, they are able to do the same with all of us most easily while we are sleeping, typically just before falling asleep, waking or in the dreaming stages of sleep. They can quite literally write themselves into our dreams.

After several nights of intense dreams of Nick and his mom's old apartment, I decided that I should sit down and try to connect with him and see just what was going on and what he wanted from me.

I waited until the house was quiet, when Javier had gone to work and Chris was off to school to try and connect with Nick. I sat down in the big chair in my living room; closed my eyes, ready to begin my meditation, only to be interrupted about thirty seconds into it. Nick was already waiting, sitting right across from me on the couch. Just as I began the meditation I heard, "Hey Denise, it's Nick," and I was immediately aware that he was in the room with me.

It's an interesting thing, dealing with spirits that have not crossed over yet and are still here on the earth plane. Even though they are communicating with me telepathically, and I'm hearing them in thought and not with my actual ears, I can still hear the sound of their voices in my mind. Once a spirit crosses over I no longer hear the sound of their voice but only their thoughts. I could hear his voice and it sounded much the same as I remembered it, only deeper now, like a man's voice as opposed to a teenager's.

Upon hearing his voice and seeing him in my home I was actually taken aback by the intensity of emotion that suddenly overcame me, seeing him after all of these years. Tears began to well up in my eyes.

"Nick, oh my God. I am so sorry Nick. I can't believe you are here..."

"Yeah, that I am dead. I'm having a hard time believing it myself," he said, shaking his head back and forth.

"What happened? I found your obituary online, but I couldn't find anything about the accident."

"I was driving home from work and it was late, between about one and two a.m. I was really tired; I had worked three days in row, double shifts at the restaurant."

He began to show me the scene from his perspective in the driver's seat. I could see that he was driving on a country road, one lane on either side. The road began a strong curve to the right and then around to the left like the bottom of the S shape. As he turned to the right and began to go around to the left, the car skidded sideways off the side of the road on the right. The road was lined with trees in a wooded area. The SUV slid sideways, passenger side, into the trees. As it hit the trees, the car bounced and leaned over on two wheels on the passenger side so that the top of the roof hits a tree which left a dent in the roof just above the passenger window. Nick was not wearing his seat belt and at the moment of impact, hit his head on the roof and broke his neck, dying almost instantly – within minutes.

the messenger

"I didn't fall asleep at the wheel, but I was tired and my reaction was slow …I was sleepy…" He paused shaking his head back and forth again. "I know that road like the back of my hand, I was just so tired and it was late. I need to talk to my wife."

"Have you been messing with my computer by any chance?"

He started laughing, "Yeah, that was me. I've been trying to get your attention all week. Will you call her? I need to talk to her…please."

"I don't know Nick, I don't think that's a good idea you know. I've been doing this along time and I have a strict rule that I don't just call people and deliver random messages. I've learned that it's not a good idea and that it doesn't usually turn out very well in most cases. Plus, it's too soon. She just had your funeral, it's too soon. You have to give it some time, give her some time."

"I need you to call Julian too, you have to call Julian. I have to talk to him. I'm worried about him. He's got it all wrong, he's off track. He doesn't believe in this, he doesn't know what he believes. He thinks that death is the end."

"Nick, I cannot call Julian. I'm sorry, but that's just not possible. I have not talked to him in twenty years. What the heck do you think he is going to think when I call him out of the blue and tell him what I do and that you are here visiting me and have a message for him? He is going to think I'm a nut, that's what he's going to think! No way, I'm sorry…no way I'm calling Julian!" I continue. "I can't do that Nick. He never knew, I never told him about me…he'll think I'm crazy. He'll never believe me anyway, you said so yourself that he doesn't believe."

"It's really cool that you can do this," Nick said. "My father told me about you and what you do. He came to meet me at the accident. I've been waiting for you to notice me for days. I have to admit if someone told me this while I was alive I wouldn't have believed you either. I probably would have laughed about it and thought you were nuts too. I'm sorry about that. You are the only one that can see me now, you and Brandon my youngest son," he continues. "He sees me, I know he does. He told Amy that I'm an angel and pointed to the corner of the room, and he was pointing at me. Amy just cried and said "Yes, Brandon, Daddy is an angel now, your guardian angel. But I was standing right there, right there with them in the room. Please Denise; please…I need to talk to Amy," he pleaded.

Chapter 14
Ghosts of Boyfriend Past

Ghosts of Boyfriend Past

Spirits have taught me through readings, that there is no such thing as failure in a relationship. We learn some of our most valuable lessons through our relationships – we are each others teachers. They remind me time and again, that we are not victims here in life we are volunteers, and we all choose to participate in our relationship experiences, regardless of their outcome. We choose our most significant partners before we are ever born into this life and we choose each other knowing full well the issues we are both coming together to work on. "Fate" and "synchronicity" coordinate the timing of our meeting in this lifetime, but believe me there is no chance in who and how we meet one another. We set it all up in advance as part of our plan.

Although we arrange our meetings and comings together, we do not necessarily write our outcomes in advance. Many of our outcomes depend on how well we learn our lessons together, if we learn them at the same pace, and if we both continue to participate in the class we are taking with one another. Sometimes one of us gets lost, sometimes both of us do. We stumble or we get off track and maybe we even decide to quit the class all together or we just graduate onto the next level of understanding and learning, and so, we separate. Many times we are not meant to be each other's one and only and we were only supposed to meet for a period of time and move on. So, whether we come together for a lifetime, a few months or a few years, all of our relationships are equally important, as they are all part of our lesson plan. I also know that we all reincarnate over and over with many of our most significant partners and family members and that we have most likely been through many lifetimes together working on these issues. In most cases, this isn't our first lifetime together and it's not likely to be our last.

The real problems come in when we don't learn or grow from our relationship experiences, and we stubbornly stumble along in our unconscious oblivion, repeating the same destructive relationship patterns. We keep changing all the players, but are stuck playing the same old game. This is when we begin to feel like the victim, and while stuck in the role of the victim, we don't realize that all along it has been us who needs to change and grow.

So, we keep looking for Mr. or Mrs. Right, thinking that when we find the right one – that special one – we will finally be happy in love and in life.

Wrong! Most of us have several possible Mr. and Mrs. Rights and when they don't work out, it is because we are either finished learning from each other what we came together to learn, or one person is growing faster than the other. Or, perhaps we are stuck in some old or dysfunctional pattern that we need to outgrow. Sometimes we are only supposed to come together for a period of time, to serve a certain purpose for one another. But, in order to change those patterns and attract the type of love that we want, we need to first be the type of person that we want to attract. We need to examine the types of people we are attracted to, how we are behaving and what our expectations are in a partner. It is most often our own selves that are looking for all the wrong things in our partner. We are often times full of unrealistic or misguided expectations and we are quick to point out what is wrong with the other instead of realizing that they are our mirror, shining back to us what we actually need to work on in ourselves.

Even then, it certainly does not lessen the pain of heartbreak and a love that is lost. There is no greater pain, whether it is through a break up or by death, than the love that is lost. The thing is though, love is never really lost. Once we are connected by love, no matter what happens in life or after death, we will always be connected by that love. It is literally like a cord of light that connects our heart to another's in eternity and from this side to the other. I have done readings for people that have been married three or four times and will invariable have a first husband come into a reading from a brief and very young marriage. A sixty-five-year-old woman who has been married several times, will often be surprised that this first husband, now passed, will come into her reading to say "Hello."

the messenger

I will explain to her that once we are linked by love, we are always linked. Love is the karmic tie that keeps us together working things out, from this lifetime and into the next.

There is nothing stronger than the bond of love, not even hate can break the bond. Because even relationships that became estranged in life, where people have disconnected completely, are angry and are no longer speaking, will reconnect again after death to sort things out and get closure on what they came here to do together. They may even choose to try it again in another life time together.

Many times, our most difficult relationships exist within our family of origin, with our parents and our siblings. This is because those family ties of love are so strong that they are the hardest to sever and therefore keep us together in the most difficult of circumstances as we try to work through our lessons. We choose to be in relationships with the difficult people in our families because we know that we would never work that hard for anyone else in our lives and we also know that they have something very important to teach us. Sometimes they teach us by showing us what to do and sometimes they teach us by showing what not to do. If it were not for the fact that someone was our parent or a child for example, we would be much more likely to throw in the towel and walk away.

In my own life, my helpers on the spirit side have taught me that I chose my mother for a reason. I have realized that my lesson with my mom is that of self-love, acceptance and self-respect. I have had to learn to give those things to myself even when I'm not receiving them from my own family. Most importantly, my mother continues to offer me the opportunity to master the lessons of unconditional love, compassion and forgiveness, which are the most important and difficult lessons that we come here in life to learn. I have learned from my relationship with her how to be strong and tough, set boundaries and to stand tall in my own power. I have learned how to stick to my guns without being intimidated. I know that if I can withstand the harshest criticism and doubt from my own mom and family, I can withstand it from anyone else because nothing any other person could ever say, would possibly be worse. She has prepared me well for the work that I do, which often comes with large doses of criticism, doubt, judgment and ridicule. After spending a lifetime of learning of how to deal with that from my own family, at this point it pretty much rolls off my back coming from any other direction. My mom has helped prepare me for a life of constant public scrutiny. She has also given me invaluable insight into the barriers I face that exist within social protocol, religious dogma, fear and ignorance. She has helped me learn to communicate my messages with people from many different levels of understanding. Although it took me a long time – close to forty years – I accept now, that I picked her to teach me to be strong, independent and self reliant. And once I figured out what I was supposed to be learning from her, I understood why I chose her to be my teacher. I also understood that I am not a victim and I finally took back my personal power that I gave away to her for so many years. Doing so allowed me to finally be free.

I have come to understand through the spirits that I work with, that we choose our family members and our relationships because the lessons that they are here learning or teaching, provide the classroom and create the circumstances for the lessons that we come here to learn. We will know, for example, before we come into this life, that one of our parents is likely to have a problem with alcohol and we agree to participate in the family with them for our mutual learning. I have also come to learn through the addiction groups that I have worked with over the years, that many families who struggle with addiction have been struggling with that lesson for several lifetimes. The child of an alcoholic may have chosen that parent for a variety of different reasons, but ultimately there is a lesson the child of an alcoholic is either here to learn from the parent or here to help the parent to learn. When we understand our lives and lessons from this perspective, we can then let go of our need to judge others and instead reclaim our personal power by taking responsibility for our part of our life experience. We have free will and we can either choose to be a helpless victim or we can choose to take control of our lives and our experience. Then we can let go of our need to be right and judge others and instead work on our own lessons, which many times are about compassion and forgiveness.

In my own life, my spirit guides constantly remind me to separate what belongs to me and what belongs to others. In other words, separate what is mine to work on and what is for others to work on. We are only responsible for our own assignment and it is very important to realize that we cannot do for another, what is theirs to do. We can offer our love, encouragement and support but for the sake of our own well being, sometimes it is necessary to step back and separate ourselves from what is for another to complete.

I think most of us have that one person – that one heartbreak – that we think we will never get over. They are the one we never forget and always wonder "What if?" What if we met at another time, or another place or in another situation? We wonder over the years, if they ever married, where they are now and how their life has turned out.

At first, after the break up, we try dating other people hoping that they will distract us long enough that we will finally forget about the one that we really love. We hope that if we fall in love with another we will stop loving the one we lost. We convince ourselves that we are better off without them and remind ourselves of all the things about them that were wrong for us. We try over and over to deny the truth that lies in our heart – that we are still deeply in love with that person. Time goes by and eventually, we do begin to forget about them and move on with our lives. Until one day, we bump into them, or an old friend and we are reminded of the mark they left on our heart and soul. We forget the horrible break-up, the nasty things that were said, and all the mistakes we made, and we reminisce about the good times and the happy moments we shared when we were in love.

As it happened, it seemed that I had just "bumped into the old friend" that would illuminate those feelings I had long ago for Julian. I found myself on a rollercoaster ride that had just begun, as the person that I had spent years trying to forget, was suddenly, as intimately connected to my life again, as he once was more than twenty years ago.

It is impossible to escape the clarity that is available to us in hindsight. I could not help but think about the things I would have done differently with Julian had I known then what I know now. But I also understand that without Julian I would not be where I am now and I would not have learned the very valuable lessons that I did during our time together. As the years went on, I met a few more men like Julian, who provided me with more opportunities to work on the lessons that I came here to learn. It is clear to me now the lessons I was taking with him and the things that he was in my life to teach me, and now, I'm only grateful for the time we shared.

It is a real testament to the irony and mystery of life that the same Julian that I spent years trying to get over and forget was now back in my life again taking center stage. It was hard to imagine even for me, that this was all happening now and I could not help but ponder the meaning of it all.

I had to admit I was curious to know how he was and what he was doing with his life, but at the same time, I was equally unsure that I really wanted to reconnect with him after all these years. So, I was faced with a choice – a tough choice – and one that really challenged me to trust my intuition and my ability to choose the best response. On the one hand, dealing with spirits was my work and accidental death circumstances are my specialty. It is what I do best and Nick was my friend once and very much like my family actually. I had loved him like my own brother and during a very pivotal coming of age time of my life. We were bonded forever by those ties of family and love.

I knew I was the only chance Nick had to have a last word with his wife and his family. However, Julian was my ex and things really didn't end on such a good note with us. As with most young lovers, our break-up was dramatic and mired in youthful angst, passion and inexperience.

After Julian initially left to move to LA, his stay wound up being brief. He came back to Baltimore about six months later for another few years before he eventually went back to LA for good. We had been separated for about two years, when I saw him again the last time.

I don't remember now, who called who first or how I knew he was back in town or why we decided to meet. It's all kind of a blur to me considering it has been close to twenty years ago now, but I do remember the last night we saw each other, very well. I was living downtown Baltimore with my two roommates from college. We had all graduated by then, but were still living together in our two-story row house. I had been working days as the Art Director for an advertising agency downtown, while still working part time as a bartender nights along with my roommates. Bartending was a fun job, very social and I made tons of cash so I kept the job until I moved to Key West. The club was an exciting place to work, it was at the time a Baltimore nightlife hot spot and it was huge. It was located downtown, right by the water across from the Inner Harbor and The Power Plant. The Original Sports Bar as it was named, featured three large inside bars, fifty large screen TVs, pool tables, dart boards and a boxing-ring that doubled as a dance floor. On the weekends and on nights with no sporting events, it was a dance club and it was frequented by lots of professional athletes and teams as they came through town to compete in their various sports. Outside, located next to the parking lot in the courtyard, was a tiki bar and sand pit where college students played beach volleyball. To get out and meet people, I had started working there after Julian and I split. I was a little shy meeting new people and so I figured the job would force me to get over my shyness, which it did. I began dating another bartender several months later. He was definitely not Mr. Right and I knew it, but he was a good diversion, for a little while, as I tried desperately to recover from my broken heart and Julian.

the messenger

I had broken things off with the bartender, months before I saw Julian that last time. I had heard through friends that Julian had been seeing someone for awhile and that he was living with her somewhere in Reisterstown, but I didn't know her. Julian and I spoke on the phone a few times before we decided to meet. I felt like I just needed to see him one more time. I wasn't sure why, but I think I just needed to see if it was really over – to see if I still loved him or if he still loved me. I wasn't sure exactly, but I was sure I needed to see him one more time.

We decided over the phone to meet at his Mom's apartment in Towson

I was really nervous to see him again after two years. It felt really strange walking up to the apartment door. My mind raced and I recalled that I could not even listen to the radio for an entire year after our break-up. Music was such a big part of his life and our life together, that after our break-up it seemed like every song I heard on the radio reminded me of him and it was unbearable. I rang the door bell and stared at the welcome mat, bouncing nervously on the balls of my feet while I waited for him to answer the door.

When he opened the door, he looked every bit as handsome as I'd remembered him. I recalled the day when those eyes could make me melt with just one certain look. His hair was still long, but straighter now and not as big and spiky on top as it used to be, as the eighties were over. He still had the same unmistakable rock and roll guitar player look though, and I thought to myself that he still looked good.

"Hi" he said looking down at me with that smile I once I loved.

He motioned for me to come in. "Hi," I responded, smiling nervously.

It's difficult to remember it all very clearly now, it was so long ago. I recall that we sat in his mom's living room for awhile and talked, although I do not remember about what. I do remember that there was something different about him that night – something was really different. Or, then again, it could have been me. There was a noticeable distance between us and he seemed detached and somewhat unfamiliar to me now. We left and went to get some dinner together in Towson. I drove, and we continued talking in the car and all through dinner. He told me all about his new band, where they were playing and about their plans to move to LA. He said that someone was interested in giving them a recording contract and that they had just finished a new album. He pulled a cassette out of his pocket at dinner and handed it to me. "Psychodrama" was the name of the band and the five guys on the cover looked like the typical rock and roll band with lots of hair and sneering.

Julian continued talking, mostly about himself and his big plans. His words ran together in a stream and I was intoxicated by his smell and the physical attraction between us was still palpable. I was sure he felt it too, like two magnets being pulled towards one another.

We drove back to the apartment after dinner and sat in the car in the parking lot for a few more minutes talking.

The next thing that I remember, we were kissing passionately. It is hard to describe how I felt in that moment. I felt attracted and repelled at the same time, like I had suddenly and unexpectedly been transported back in time to high school again. I could feel my soul, my heart and my body being sucked back in, as if I was being pulled back into an addiction or was under a spell. I felt like I was losing control as I felt all the old emotions flooding back in like a tidal wave. I was consumed by his energy and it was wonderful, intoxicating and at the same time it was terrifying. I had spent two years trying to forget that feeling – trying to forget how I felt when I was with him and how he broke my heart – and now here I was, right back in his arms…again.

The hair was rising on the back of my neck and I began to feel overcome with a sense of panic. I felt like I couldn't breathe – like I was suffocating and that I might faint. It was a familiar feeling and the same way I felt when he left for LA to become a rock star. The emotional resonance was kicking in, serving as a reminder of what I was getting myself back into. With his arms wrapped around me, his lips pressed against mine, the smell of his familiar cologne consuming me, I suddenly came to my senses, and snapped out of his love spell.

I pulled back, caught my breath and stared at him – straight into his eyes, searching his soul. The feeling wasn't there. He felt far away and distant. I couldn't do it. I just couldn't be with him again, although I wanted to more than anything. I felt like I couldn't breathe, like I was suffocating and I was clear. I couldn't be with him now or ever.

"Julian, I can't do this. What are we doing? Why are we doing this? You are living with a girl and I…well I might be moving soon." I paused. "It's over. We can't see each other again."

I began to think about the fact that he was living with his girlfriend and kissing me in the car and what that meant and said about him. It all just didn't feel right; he had seemed so emotionally distant and cold. As much as I'd wanted it too, none of it felt right. He was not the same person anymore and for that matter, neither was I.

the messenger

He sat quietly for a moment, looked at me, smiled a little and said "Okay". That was it, "okay" and just like that, he opened the door and got out of the car. That was the last time I had seen him, and now I was being asked to open a chapter in my life, I had long ago closed.

Chapter 15
A Haunting Message

A Haunting Message

Ever since I can remember, as a young girl I have always loved and had a fascination for anything to do with haunted houses and ghost stories. I still love a good scary ghost movie even though they never scare me, and I get excited by any reports of a haunting. Professionally, I am sometimes commissioned to investigate hauntings and although I have met many people in life that I have found to be quite scary, I can honestly say that I have never once met a spirit of whom I felt afraid. In my work with Prospect Hope Crisis Center, where we received referrals directly from local law enforcement agencies and the medical examiner's office, I often read for those who lost loved ones in violent crimes. Homicides and domestic violence were common in those groups. I was also confronted many times working in those groups with the spirit of a murderer wanting to come through and speak to the victim's family. In every single case, the perpetrator was filled with regret, remorse and tremendous anguish over his wrong doings. There is so much misunderstanding about spirits and haunting, which has been perpetuated by Hollywood and even religion. In my extensive professional experience as a medium, working with the spirit world on a daily basis, I have found that in most cases, spirits do not want to scare us or hurt us and are merely just trying hard to get our attention. There is one particular case that I worked on in my private practice that continues to be one of the most memorable readings I've ever done for a haunting. It was eye opening and inspiring and the spirit in the reading taught me so much about our life after death and the real meanings behind the concepts of Heaven and Hell.

I received an email from a sixty-three year old woman who was terrified by some supernatural activity that had been occurring and escalating in her home. She reported to me that she had seen lights and shadows around her house and had heard things rattling downstairs in the kitchen at night. She also reported that her husband who had formerly professed to be a non-believer in ghosts had even admitted to seeing them too. I became more concerned when she began to speak of her four year old granddaughter who had recently begun to report seeing and speaking with spirits in her house. The woman, who told me that she was a Christian, had even had a priest come to the home to bless the house and try to cast out the spirits, but that things had only gotten worse since his visit.

Her greatest concern was for her granddaughter, who stayed with her quite often. She was concerned that the ghost might hurt her. The woman reported to me that she had been awakened in the middle of the night on a few occasions, feeling someone touching her and moving around in the bed. Now granted, I can get some *way out there* emails from people from time to time, but the tone of her email just did not strike me that way. She seemed rational and intelligent but at the same time very scared. She asked if I would come to her home and offered to pay for my time and expenses and fly me to Louisiana where she lived. She and her husband had recently retired and had just built their dream house there and she did not want to leave the house, but was desperate for help.

We exchanged a few more emails and I advised her that I did not believe it was necessary for me to fly out to her home and that I would like to try and "look into" this by phone first. She agreed, and we scheduled an appointment. I asked her to be in the house for the reading so I could really tune in to the energy there and what was happening.

As I began the reading, I delivered a few messages to her first from her father who was passed. Then as I began to tune in to the house, I immediately became aware of the spirit of a black male that was in his early to mid-thirties when he passed. I was also aware that Barbara, my client, and her husband, George, were not black, but were Caucasian. The spirit told me that he was the one that had been haunting their house and that he was there for her husband. He then showed me her husband in a policeman's uniform. I asked her if he was and she stated that he had been for twenty-five years but was now retired. She went on to tell me that he currently was working part-time for the medical examiners office. I explained to her that as a result of the amount of death and tragedy they

the messenger

are often exposed to in their daily work, it is actually quite common for police, paramedics and firefighters to have experiences with spirits or even sometimes have them hang around.

The black male in spirit went on to describe and show to me, in great detail, a scene that he told me happened in 1979. I saw a low-income housing project which I believed to be in the northern part of Florida or Georgia (it was later validated to be Florida). He showed me the cops coming in cars and surrounding the apartment building, and then I watched a young, black male run out of one of the apartments trying to escape. Then I saw clearly, a policeman shooting him.

He continued to tell me that this prompted a huge investigation into the police department as the people and media claimed the shooting was racially motivated. He told me that the young black male was unarmed and that three of the policemen lost their jobs because of the incident. After describing in detail all of what this man was showing me to Barbara, sounding puzzled and confused, she said that she had no idea what I was talking about and could not verify any of the information or details that he was giving to me.

"Barbara, I tell you what," I said to her. "I really believe this man is here for your husband, not you. I believe he is connected to your husband and wants to speak with him. Do you think he would be open to this?"

"I don't know," she paused, "I'm not sure. He knows I'm calling you and he agreed to pay for the reading for my birthday present, but I don't think he really believes in any of this."

"Okay then, well just do me a favor okay? Play this recording for your husband and if any of what I said makes any sense to him at all, have him contact me and I will read for him at no charge. Okay?" I asked her. "I'm sorry but I really think this man is trying to get through to your husband and without him, I cannot make sense of this spirit's story. I really need to speak with your husband."

Well a few days went by and I received an email from George. It seemed that George knew exactly what I was talking about, not only the black male, but the whole incident. He said in his email that he could not believe it, as the scene that I described on the recording in detail had happened when he was living in Florida and ten years before he met his wife. He also told me that he never told her about any of it. He said he never believed in this sort of thing, but confessed in the email, that there was no way I could have known about all the things I was describing to him. I could tell he was pretty astounded by what he had heard on the recording and in fact, he said so. I had made the assumption after the reading, that the scene the black man was showing me was of his own death, but I was about to find out that my assumption had been wrong. We set up an appointment and I was really looking forward to the reading, anxious to get to the bottom of what was going on with the spirit and why he was haunting the couple.

   George came on the phone and without telling me the story of what happened, or any of the details, he again validated to me that all of the information that was on the recording, made perfect sense to him. He told me he knew exactly what I was speaking of and was anxious to hear more of what I and the spirit had to say. I explained to George, in terms that I knew he would understand from being a Police Detective, that for me this was like walking into a room with a table that had five pieces of evidence on it. I told him that although I can describe clearly and in detail what I am seeing and what the evidence looks like, without reading the criminal file and knowing the full story, I do not know what the evidence means and how to put it all into context. I told him that was why I needed to speak with him, so he could make sense of what the spirit was showing me. The explanation appealed to him and he understood exactly what I was saying.

   The spirit of the black man was there waiting with me before I ever got on the phone with George and he told me that the scene he was showing me of the young black man getting shot was not him, but his son. He told me that his son had not been killed, but was in jail for life. As I relayed his messages to George, the spirit continued to tell me that he, the spirit, had been a very bad man in life and that he had been involved in gangs and drugs and had killed several people. Although I was not at all afraid of him now as a spirit, I became acutely aware of what a very bad man he had been in his life and the evil acts that he had committed while here. I could sense his brutality and the violent nature of his crimes. However, as I met with him in spirit, I was also profoundly aware of the intense amount of regret and remorse he had for his actions, and the life that he had chosen to live. I was also unquestionably certain, that he was in no way an evil spirit. He had been in life, a man living in ignorance with vast misunderstanding, who had gotten very off track and who had indeed chosen the wrong path and done some very evil things. He was not an evil soul though, and of that, I was very certain.

   He went on to confess, with tremendous regret, that it was his fault that

the messenger

his two sons had turned out the way they had. He told me that they never had a chance. He said they had been raised to be brutal and to be killers and he even showed me his son at eight years old smoking marijuana. I continued sharing all of this with George. I cannot express adequately with words, the immensity of regret and remorse for his life choices that this spirit carried with him. He understood fully what the consequences of his actions were on those he had victimized, their families and his own family. Then he said the most amazing thing, and as I was about to find out, it was the main message that he came to deliver to George – it was his reason for haunting their house.

"George, he is telling me that he came to tell you, thank you. He says that he wants to thank you for saving his son's life." I was puzzled by this message and I assumed that he must have meant that by putting his son in jail he saved him from dying at a young age from living a life of crime as a gangster.

I could here George getting choked up and emotional on the other end of the line. "George, are you okay? Do you understand that? Does that message make sense to you?"

He cleared his throat as he struggled to maintain his composure. I waited for his reply.

"Yes, yes I do." He cleared his throat again.

"He is telling me that you paid a heavy price for your choice. He said that you took a lot of heat from your colleagues in the police department and that you were called on to testify against some of them. He says that you had to testify against some of your peers that were brought up on charges for racial misconduct. He said the shooting caused a huge media event and prompted an investigation that led to charges against the department. He is telling me that for some reason your role in all of this has been a great and heavy burden that you have carried on your shoulders for many years. He says that you were made a scapegoat in some way. He is telling me that he came here today to relieve that burden and thank you again for saving his son's life. He wants you to know how important your decision was to his son's life. He says that you are a very good and admirable man. He says that he is really sorry that you have had to carry this burden for so long."

I waited for George to respond. A few moments of silence passed and then George cleared his throat and began to explain to me what happened. He said that he was the officer that shot the young man that was this spirits son. He said the night before the shooting, the son, who was nineteen at the time, had brutally stabbed to death his pregnant girlfriend. He stabbed her seventeen times. When they went to make the arrest, he tried to flee and because they were in a downtown area, George was concerned they would lose him in the city streets. George said that the man was considered very dangerous and he was a known gangster with a violent criminal record. He told me that in those situations, the officers are trained to shoot to kill. He told me that as the young man ran out the front door of the apartment, he had a clear shot and because he was a very good marksman, he could have easily shot him point-blank in the chest and killed him. He went on to tell me that he didn't kill him, but instead made a conscious, split second decision to spare his life. He shot him once in the shoulder and another time in the thigh to bring him down and into custody. George confirmed to me that he is currently in jail and serving life in prison, as is his brother for a separate incident. They were the only two sons of the spirit.

George continued to tell me that he had shot two people in his career and this man was one of them. He said that, although as a police officer he was trained to shoot and even kill, that each shooting was very upsetting to him. And even though he did not kill the young man, he reported that he had come close to having a nervous breakdown over the shooting and the controversy that ensued following the incident. He said the only person he had ever confided this to was a priest, shortly after the shooting.

I went on to share some other messages from George's father and grandfather that left the reading on a lighter note. It was obvious to me the enormity of the impact that the messages from this spirit carried with George and the peace and closure that it provided to him. George was relieved, amazed and incredibly grateful to me for the messages, as he thanked me several times and let me know how much this had meant to him. His father went on to tell me that George could see spirits too, and when I asked him why he didn't tell me, he said that he has never really told anyone before. He said that he was not scared by it, but was actually sort of matter of fact about his own spirit sightings and chalked it up as coming with the job. He told me for the most part he just ignored them, which I found pretty amusing.

So, it is important to recognize and understand that this spirit was haunting this couple for the sole purpose of delivering a very important and healing message – a message that was just as important for the spirit's healing and growth, as it was for George. His style of getting his message through was merely a reflection of his consciousness and of the man he had been in his life. He was a man that had lived his life using fear and intimidation as a means to control and manipulate others, so it was by fear that he felt would be the most effective way to get the attention of Barbara. He also apologized to George in the reading for scaring his wife. He said that he really didn't want to scare her but he knew it was the only way that she would call me so that he could get his message through to George. Otherwise, he knew that George would have never have called me on his own. It was the best way that he knew to get his message through, and it worked!

So I have learned time and again, that most things are rarely as they appear. There is always something much bigger going on behind the scenes of our every day lives and even behind the scenes of a haunting. In this case, and as we will all do when we cross over, this spirit, reviewed his life and was shown how all of his thoughts, actions and choices affected all of those around him and in turn, the ripple affect that they created in the world. Not only was he "shown" how his life had affected others, but he had to "feel" how he had made others feel.

This spirit explained to me in the reading that he will have to endure feeling all of the fear, pain and suffering that he had caused others in his life until he makes things right with everyone of them and they forgive him. He will do his best from the spirit side and also in his next life, to make things right as much as he can with the people he harmed. He told me that he will only be released from his suffering and having to re-live the consequences of his actions when the people that he hurt finally forgive him.

Forgiveness is a common theme in readings and is one of the most important lessons that we come here to learn. It is most important to understand that forgiveness is as important to the victim as it is the victimizer – whether they are alive or now in spirit. Forgiveness is also a two way street and it is necessary for both parties to let go, heal and move on. Forgiveness is what releases us from the karmic ties that connect us to each other in toxic ways. Karma is commonly misunderstood and is not a system of cosmic punishment. It is simply lessons that we came here to learn, or what we have earned through the consequences of our choices and actions, in a current or past lifetime. Forgiveness is the ONLY way that we can release ourselves from the toxic ties that bind us to others in unhealthy ways. So, forgiveness is not something you give to another, it is something you give to yourself, and that in turn, also helps the other grow in understanding and spiritual awareness.

It is also very important to understand that although we may not always find "justice" and accountability in this lifetime, none of us can escape accountability for long. Eventually, we will ALL have to accept responsibility for our actions and will have to make things right with all of those we have harmed, whether intentionally or unintentionally, however big or small that consequence. I'm told by Spirit, the ultimate goal of life here, is to become more conscious of our affect on others and by doing so, learn to develop the higher qualities of empathy and compassion. Empathy and compassion are the highest forms of unconditional and "true" love.

I must point out here that the spirit that contacted George, is very clear that the forgiveness he needed and sought does not come from God – releasing him in one fell swoop from all of his pain and suffering. He was very clear, and I have heard this from countless other spirits over the years, that the forgiveness he was seeking – that we all will seek – must come from those he harmed. He also made it clear that as part of his growth and learning, he must make things right with the people that he harmed and he can only do that by taking responsibility for his actions.

Gratitude is also VERY important for us on this side and those on the spirit side, as it is the way that we honor and recognize the caring and selfless actions of another. It was most important for this spirit to express his gratitude to George for saving his son's life, which in turn allowed his son to continue with learning his lessons here, in this life. The spirit recognized that by George making the decision to spare his young son's life, he was giving his son a chance to make some things right in his life, even if he had to do so from a prison cell. If George had taken his son's life, he would have had to come back and start all over again from scratch in another lifetime. This way, at least he still had some time in this life to understand the error of his ways, realize how his actions affected others and have a chance to make some amends.

This spirit provided a perfect example of what "Hell" really is. We create our own Heaven or Hell through the choices we make and the consequences of our actions on others. When we cross over to the spirit side, we will all review our lives once we arrive. We will be shown how our life, actions and choices affected all the other lives we touched, for good or for ill, and we will see the ripple affect that we created. So, by the same token, if we live our life with love and compassion for others, making choices that reflect that, then we get to receive back all the love and joy we spread and relive all of the good we created in the world for eternity on the spirit side of life.

the messenger

We will not only see how we affected others in positive ways but we will also get to feel the love we created and perpetuated through our caring and compassion. So as you can see in the case of the cop haunting, this spirit was in no way evil or trying to harm this couple. He was just trying to get their attention, desperately trying to make amends and set things right.

Chapter 16
The "Grateful" Dead

The "Grateful" Dead

"*Sometimes the lights all shinin on me; other times I can barely see. Lately it occurs to me what a long, strange trip it's been*" – The Grateful Dead

"*Truckin got my chips cashed in…keep truckinnnn…*" blared from the iPod alarm clock on the nightstand. I practically jumped up out of my bed, quite suddenly jolted from a very deep sleep. My heart pounded as I tried to regain my equilibrium and consciousness. The bedroom would have been pitch black if it were not for the light streaming from the video display of my iPod. I reached over and hit the light that illuminates the alarm clock to see that it was 4:34am. The Grateful Dead was still playing as I rolled over to see that Javier was still sound asleep beside me in the bed.

The room was actually quite bright now as the iPod illuminated my small bedroom. Just as I rolled back over to turn off the music and go back to sleep, I saw Nick sitting with one leg crossed over the other in the chair right next to the nightstand on my side of the bed. He was wearing the same tie-dyed Grateful Dead shirt that I remembered him wearing when we were in high school. As I recall, he was a big fan of The Dead back then. As I reached over to turn the music off, I made a mental note of the fact that the alarm had not been set for 4:34 and had not been turned "on."

"Jesus Nick! You just scared the crap out of me!" With the music now off, the light illuminating the alarm clock still lit the room dimly with a bluish white glow and I could clearly see Nick laughing in the chair.

"Boo!" he said with a big grin on his face.

"Ha Ha, that's very funny!" I replied sarcastically.

It had been just about four months since Nick's accident and he had been visiting me at home on and off over the course of those months. Just as I had remembered him, Nick still had a great sense of humor and seemed to really get a kick out of playing practical jokes on me. He found it quite entertaining and amusing to turn the stereo in my living room on in the middle of the night, or turn my computer off and on when I was working and even enjoyed playing with Sage. Javier was also becoming quite accustomed to Nick's presence and mentioned one morning in passing that the light on the night table on his side of the bed had turned on in the middle of the night. When I replied with, "It did?" He just answered "yeah, I just got up and turned it off." He added, "Must be your friend again."

Nick had been pleading with me for months to contact his brother Julian and said that he really needed to talk to him before he left. He would pop in and out of my home randomly and particularly liked to mess with my computer, as I'm sure he knew it really pissed me off.

I'm on my computer practically all day long as most days I work from home, so when my computer is not working properly it creates a complete disruption of my work and daily life. In the first month after Nick's passing I took my computer to the Geek Squad on three separate occasions insisting that something must be wrong as it kept shutting off and turning back on. I'm quite certain the tech guy thought I was nuts, as he told me that he would leave it turned on all day while he was at work and it never shut off once. Finally, after I picked it up for the third time he said to me "I don't know Ms. Lescano, you must have the poltergeist computer," shaking his head back and forth with a slight chuckle.

As I picked up my computer and headed for the door, I thought to myself, *"yeah, you have no idea how true that is,"* I shook my own head back and forth. I immediately proceeded home to yell at Nick and tell him to stop messing with my PC! Most people don't know that it is incredibly easy for spirits to mess with electronics. As spirits are bundles of energy it is quite easy for them to affect anything that is electrical, like house phones, cell phones, car radios and TV's. Sometimes they do it intentionally to get our attention and other times they do it quite accidentally. Depending on the strength of their energy and often the intensity of their emotional energy, they can inadvertently short things out just by being in the room. I cannot begin to count how many lights, timers, appliances and other electronics I have had to replace over the years. I am quite certain it is a much higher amount than most people and it gets to the point of being almost comical

the messenger

sometimes. Javier and Chris have witnessed first hand spirits messing with our electronics. My son Chris had always been very close to his dad's cousin. When he passed a few years back, at the young age of forty-four with cancer, my son came home from school every day for a week to have the TV in his room turn on at 4:14. I knew it was his cousin Chris, who my son was named after, stopping by to say "*Hi*," and let Chris know he was okay. It was no coincidence either that the iPod turned on playing The Grateful Dead as it was one of Nick's favorite songs when we were kids.

    A few weeks after Nick died, I contacted his widow Angie, after I found her name and the town where they lived in the obituary. I got her phone number through directory assistance and I very politely introduced myself to her by phone. To my surprise, she knew who I was, even though we had never met. She and Nick began dating several years after Julian and I had split, but she told me that she had heard all about me and had seen photos of Julian and me at the prom. Apparently Julian's Mom still had a picture of us together, framed on a coffee table in her living room. I expressed my condolences for Nick's passing, told her how much I was fond of him and that I had thought of him like a brother. She thanked me and seemed remarkably composed, it being so soon after his death. I told her that I did not want to take up her time, but that I was trying to find out how to get in touch with Julian. I offered to leave my number and email and asked if she would pass it on to Julian and ask him to contact me, not wanting to ask for his number and put her on the spot. However, she cheerfully offered to give me his number and email and insisted that she thought he would be really happy to hear from me after all these years. Never saying a word about what I do or Nick's visits, I thanked her and hung up the phone. Over the next few months Julian and I exchanged several emails. He seemed genuinely excited to hear from me and in spite of the tragic circumstances behind our reconnecting, his emails were cheerful and friendly. We caught up with each others lives and I sent him a picture of Chris and told him that I was married and living in Florida. He in turn told me that he had not married and was working as a comic book artist. From the sounds of it, he had become a very successful and accomplished illustrator and had worked on several very big film projects that I knew of.

    All the while Nick was asking me to deliver his message to Julian, and all the while I refused. As I stated earlier, it becomes very difficult for me to read another person once I have become emotionally involved with them. The reason being is that their life and lessons are now intertwined with mine and I am not allowed to see everything in my own life as I am here to learn and grow just like everyone else. So, if someone I'm involved with has lessons to learn that are connected to the lessons that I am here to learn, Spirit will not reveal to me what is going on with them no matter how much I plead. Although the spirit world is eager to offer us guidance and direction in our lives, they cannot and will not, do anything that will interfere with our free will or compromise our learning process by giving us the answers to our lessons. So, try as I might, I could not get a read on Julian at all, about how he felt about life after death or what he might believe about spirits and mediums. Finally, after exchanging about a half dozen or so emails and establishing a friendly rapport I decided to send him an email with a link to my web site and let him see for himself what I do.

It was a difficult decision for me, as I had never told Julian that I was psychic or could see spirits and I'm not sure how much I really understood about my own abilities at the time we were together. So telling him now, after all these years, stirred up quite a bit of anxiety and insecurity for me. I was quite sure he would probably think that I was crazy and I that would never hear from him again. On the other hand, I did hold out hope that when he saw the credible and respectable organizations that I worked with, he might think again.

Several days went by with no word and my stomach was tied up in knots waiting and wondering. I even started the email with "I know this is probably going to sound crazy, but..." assuming that he was going to think I was. After all, what person wouldn't think so? It was like something out of a movie; high school sweet heart contacts old beau after twenty-five years to tell him that she is being haunted by his recently deceased brother. Yes, even to me it sounded crazy and stranger than fiction. I took every chance I could to remind Nick of this as well, certain that he had lost perspective now being on the spirit side, of how crazy this would all sound to his brother.

So as it came to pass, that at precisely 4:34 a.m. my time that same morning, Julian sent me an email from LA. It was 1:34 a.m. his time.

"Julian just sent you an email," Nick said with a grin.

Wide awake now, I got up and closed the door to the bedroom, so as not to wake Javier. And, I could not help but wonder what he might think at the thought of me getting up in the middle of the night to read an email from an ex-boyfriend. I knew that I would probably not like it if the roles were reversed. However, this was different, and these were very unusual circumstances. I saw no other choice really, as it had become very clear to me that Nick was not leaving until I contacted Julian.

Julian's email was thoughtful and kind and he assured me that he did not think I was crazy. He told me that although he was "respectfully skeptical," he was curious. I replied to the email and asked if he had read on my web site that I specialize in working with sudden and accidental death and if he had seen the organizations that I worked with? In the next email he said that yes he had seen that and remarked that he found that very interesting and seemed surprised. I replied again that I really would like to speak with him on the phone and that I really felt like we needed to talk. I did not say anything about doing a reading or delivering messages from Nick or that I was receiving visits from him, just that I'd like to chat and catch up. I felt as if it were best to just get reacquainted first. We exchanged several more emails and over the course of about six weeks, set up three different times to talk by phone only for Julian to send me an email with an excuse to cancel at the last minute. I grew increasingly frustrated and could not help but feel irritated by his indecision, as familiar old feelings from our relationship began to kick in. It was a very difficult task that Nick was asking me too do, because I found it very challenging to separate my personal bias and feelings for Julian from the work that I was trying to do for Nick. I must admit I found it all terribly confusing to say the least.

Meanwhile, as all of this was going on between Julian and I, I received an email from Angie, Nick's widow. It seemed that Julian and given her my web site. She sent me a polite and curious email telling me that she had no idea that I was a medium and that she found it very interesting. I replied and told her that if she wanted, I would be happy to read for her at no charge and that I would like to do that for Nick. Well about a month went by, but she eventually took me up on the offer. I had still not spoken to Julian and out of frustration I decided to quit emailing him all together. I could not help but wonder if he was waiting to hear from Angie and what she thought about me before he decided if he wanted to speak with me. I still wasn't sure if his hesitation was because of what I did for work or our past history together.

The reading with Angie went really well. I asked Nick before hand to make sure that he brought through some very specific, very personal things that I would have no way of knowing from my involvement with their family. I knew that he would really have to blow her away for her to believe that this was real. I understood that she was skeptical. Nick did a great job and I felt confident by the end of our session that she was a true believer and knew I was connecting with Nick.

Nick brought through several tidbits of personal information like her favorite martini, the bar they used to like to hang out in together and he told me that they at one time lived together in St. Thomas before they were married. He also went on to tell me that when he proposed to her, he proposed on the beach with a ring that he had made out of tin foil from the bar, because he didn't have enough money to buy her a ring. She validated that it was true and told me he eventually did buy her a real ring. There were several other very personal messages for her and his kids, that were from the heart and she was emotional and obviously touched. His message for her was not about forgiveness, or to set the record straight or even deliver some unknown piece of information as spirits often do. His message was only to let her know how much he loved her and missed her, that he was okay and still with her and the kids. He told her that he had been trying to let her know that by turning on the stereo in her house in the middle of the night to which she acknowledged and laughed about. He also made sure to tell her that when she was sleeping one night with her son and he woke up yelling "Daddy" and pointing excitedly to an empty corner in the bedroom, that it was indeed him really standing there in the room. Ayden, his son, being only four, could see his daddy and I explained to Angie how this is common among young children. Nick also brought through a few messages which he asked her to give to Julian. She thanked me several times and I hung up the phone feeling grateful for the chance to give this gift to Nick. After I got off the phone, Nick thanked me and I felt good that I was able to do this for him. I could actually "feel" his gratitude and I had not seen him so much at peace since his death.

Julian had passed on my web site to his mom and I heard from her almost a year later, doing a reading for as well. She also seemed skeptical, however was excited to hear from me. I think that for many people that knew me before I was a medium, as a young girl, it must be difficult to believe that I became the person I am today. Nick's mom and I spent close to three hours on the phone, reminiscing about the fun we had all had together.

Sadly, I never really got through to Julian in spite of my best efforts to do so. We did eventually speak on the phone, catching up on what we were both up to now and we had a very nice conversation about Nick. Talking to Julian again felt like talking to a very dear old friend and our conversation was natural and easy and it felt to me as if no time had passed by. It was strangely familiar and poignant as I recalled so many years earlier the first time that we had met and I had thought to myself that it felt like I had known Julian forever. I offered to read for Julian one day if he would like and connect him with Nick, telling him that I really thought Nick would like to speak with him.

Curiously, or maybe not so, I never heard from Julian again after that. Just as he had done so many times before, he simply disappeared from my life. I sent him a few more emails regarding an upcoming class reunion that I was involved in but received no reply. To this day, I'm not sure why I never heard from Julian again. But, I have considered that perhaps it was all too much for him, the passing of his brother then hearing from me and about what I do. I wondered if he was still skeptical that I really could see and speak to Nick or if the idea scared him. I could not dismiss the thought that he might have just decided that I was crazy and written me off. I also wondered if maybe it was his feelings about me and our past together that prompted him to sever ties with me once again. I would like to believe that perhaps hearing that Nick was okay through Angie and his mom, was enough for Julian to know. For now I just have to accept that I may never know why I never heard from him again. I also understand that connecting with those who have passed onto the spirit side does not appeal to everyone. I know I have given my best for Nick and it is now up to him to complete the task. Interestingly, after my conversation with Julian by phone, Nick never appeared in my home again and I knew that he had finally gone home.

I have heard from him a few times since then from the spirit side and he has even helped me write this story, particularly the chapters about him and Julian. Where my memory failed me, he impressed me with thoughts and memories that I had long forgotten of the times we had all shared. He also came up with the clever title of this chapter and gave me The Grateful Dead quote. I can only assume that there is a message in the lyrics to the friends that he left behind, who will understand it when they read this book.

For me, I cannot help but acknowledge what a long and sometimes strange trip this has been for me. I pondered for many months the meaning of Nick coming back into my life in such a profound and sudden way. I could not fail to recognize the significance of such an encounter and the chain of events that it caused. It was because of Nick's death that I was reunited once again with so many childhood friends that I had become disconnected from so many years ago.

At first I thought the reason might have something to do with Julian. I thought that it was all happening in order for Nick to get through to Julian and his family. And, in some respects it was. Upon delivering Nick's messages to his mom and wife, he was able to let go and go home. He just needed to say "*Goodbye.*" But I still could not understand why I had reconnected with Julian after all of this time. I wondered why, even though Nick was never able to deliver his message to Julian through me, that once Julian and I spoke on the phone, he was finally able to go home.

I eventually figured out that Julian and I must have needed to reconnect for another reason that had to do with us and not Nick. Nick was just playing the match-maker, trying to get us to reconnect. Still, I couldn't understand why it would be at this point in my life.

Chapter 17
the messenger

the messenger

It took me awhile to assimilate all that had happened and to really understand the message that Nick had come back into my life to deliver. At first I thought the message was for Julian but later came to realize the message was a gift to me from Nick for helping him. This time the message was for the messenger – for me. His message, it turned out, was part of the inspiration for this book.

I have been trying to write this book for years. I knew what I wanted to say and some of the stories that I wanted to tell. I knew the message that Spirit wanted me to deliver through the book, but I could never really decide how to present the story. I had thought about other books that I have read from other mediums over the years, and I knew that I really wanted to write something different. The year that Nick came back into my life again, 2008, was a particularly difficult year for me and I was struggling to keep my morale up. Like so many others, Javier and I were facing a possible foreclosure, as the real estate market in south Florida plummeted and we watched our home value drop sixty percent. I was in the midst of wrangling with the bank and dealing with my attorney, trying to work out a loan modification, when Nick reappeared in my life. It was still unclear to me, during that summer however, whether we would be successful with our loan modification or wind up in foreclosure, like most people in the area already had. I loved my home – it was my dream home – and the thought of losing it was heartbreaking to us both. We had poured our heart and soul into its walls, painting and decorating. And, I had enjoyed countless days gardening and landscaping our beautiful tropical garden. I went to sleep every night for six months wondering if we would have a home the following month. To add insult to injury, Chris, who had just turned thirteen, was really missing his dad who had moved back to the northeast, and decided that he wanted to try living with him. Nothing was going to change his mind. I knew that he really needed the time with his dad, so reluctantly I let him go and try it out. I was heartbroken though and could not help but feel like my family was being split-up, once again, just as it had been during my divorce. Although he wound up staying only a short time before he eventually came back, anyone who is a parent knows how devastating it was for me to let him go

Yes, there are times in all of our lives, even mine, that try our soul. We face trials that test our faith and courage and require us to trust in forces that we have faith are there looking out for us and our loved ones. This was one of those times in my life. Being so far from my son was nothing less than unbearable and I found it difficult to sleep at night without knowing that he was safe at home with me, in his bed. It was a time that Spirit was teaching me the meaning of trust. As the world, the economy and even my own home-life seemed to be spiraling out of control, it was a time that all I had to count on was my trust in the spiritual forces that I knew were helping me.

Life has an uncanny way of wearing us down sometimes, causing us to wonder why we even bother with it all. I'm no different and have had those moments in my own life when I question why and how much longer I must endure something. Of course knowing what I know about life and why we are here, I can intellectually and spiritually understand it all, but that does not necessarily lessen the pain and suffering of my own human experience. It was a very difficult time when Nick popped in to my home and my life. I was mentally, emotionally, and physically exhausted and there was no end in sight. What I eventually came to realize about Nick's message was that, this time, it was meant for me. I was feeling dispirited and discouraged and wondering if and when it would all end. Being the survivor that I have always been, I was not about to give up, but I was beginning to wonder why I should even bother anymore. As I look back now, I have come to realize that Nick helped me to reconnect with my youth and in turn, rediscover the idealism it held. He reminded me of the true and simple heart of a young girl who once so innocently and naively loved Julian. He helped me recall within those memories my purest intentions, my sincere heart, and to remember and identify it's most natural and authentic impulses. He helped me to remember who I was, where I came from and who I am now, and in doing so, allowed me to reconnect with my own inner-child. He reminded me of a simpler time, when life was less complicated and as a result, he enabled my optimistic and more honorable side to look past all of the challenges, disappointments and set backs that we all tend to see so easily and get stuck on from time to time.

The high school reunion was the icing on the cake and was almost a year to the date of his death. Although Julian did not attend, all of our closest friends were there; Ellie, Chris and Lindsey, our buddy JJ and David the singer in Julian's band. Although Todd Baker was in the class above us he came and brought his two side kicks Louie and Paul, whom I was equally excited to see. The party, extending over a weekend, much to my surprise, was hosted one night by David at the Old Original Sports Bar that I had been a bartender. Talk about a blast from the past. We all had a great time and everyone expressed their gratitude to Ellie and me for organizing it. It seemed everyone was weary from the affects of the recession one way or another and the destabilization of life as we had all come to know it. The reunion allowed us all to reconnect to that simpler time, when life was less complicated and we were young and full of optimism. Our hearts were filled, as we caught up with one another and reminisced about the good old days. It reminded me of how important it is for all of us to not lose touch with that young, innocent and tender part of ourselves. I also knew that Nick had played a big part in all of us coming together again for the reunion.

On a very personal note, for me it was somehow the last piece to a big puzzle I had been trying to put together my whole life. Until the reunion, I had been living out two separate identities my entire life. I had the life before anyone knew I was a medium and the life after. I had spent a lifetime hiding who I was and what I could do and pretending to be normal.

Although I was now working professionally as a psychic and medium, I was still careful to keep my two identities separate as much as I could, only telling old friends and colleagues I was doing "consulting" work. Needless to say, I was more than a little nervous that I was now in essence "coming out of the closet" to my old friends. I could not help but wonder how they would react and what they would think.

Since the advent of the internet and Facebook I was sure that everyone knew what I was and I also imagined there was a lot of curiosity about me and my work. However, much to my surprise, no one really cared much and regarded me just as they as always did – as their friend. It was a nostalgic and joyful reunion and everyone who attended felt it. And although we had all grown and changed, in many ways, it was as if no time had passed at all and we were just as connected as we'd been twenty-five years earlier.

Nick's message reminded me once again, that we are not separated and we are all connected to one another from now to eternity. I'm reminded that although we may be separated for a time by distance or years or death, we are never really separated at all. The separation is an illusion and that once we are connected by the bonds of love and friendship, we are bonded for eternity. Nick had always lived his life in a big and bold way that inspired so many others. So, it was only fitting that he would leave all of those whose lives he touched, including mine, with an admiration for his love of life.

Spirit has taught me through many readings that we all choose how and when we are going to die as it is the way that we will travel home. There are truly no accidents. They have also explained to me that when a person chooses to die young and suddenly, they usually choose to do so to magnify their message or the legacy they left behind. I always use the Crocodile Hunter, Steve Irwin, as a great example of this. When I heard the news of his sudden passing from being stabbed in the chest by a sting-ray while shooting his TV show, I immediately thought, what a perfect and appropriate way for him to go! It was a freak accident, as sting-rays are not aggressive towards people. It made me think, "How brilliant!" Through his death, he was able to draw so much more attention to his cause for wildlife appreciation and conservation. Within his untimely and ironic death, he actually planned the perfect publicity stunt for his life's work and anyone who watched him knew the complete and total passion he had for it. He lived his life and decidedly died for it.

I have never once talked to a spirit on the spirit side that wanted to come back into their life. They always want to stay where they are. Although they miss the loved ones they have left behind, they are happy to be home. They have told me over and again that the spirit side has only unconditional love, compassion and forgiveness, and that however we might imagine God to be, God is only Love with a capacity that is endless and infinite.

I would like to leave you with a story of a very dear friend of mine who passed away suddenly in his sleep, Alan Arcieri. Like me, Alan was also a medium and a close and cherished colleague and friend. He was a source of unfailing support for me, as I learned to walk this path. He taught me how to trust again, for which I will be eternally grateful.

the messenger

I met Alan at the time that I had come out of the closet about my abilities and I had begun to work more publicly in my new profession. It was also just about the same time that I had begun doing the support group work. Alan was nine years my senior and had been working full time as a medium a few years longer than I had. He had also been reading for people in group settings for awhile. At the time I met Alan, I was still struggling with my feelings about being in the public eye, under such a microscope of scrutiny and doubt. I was just learning to deal with the challenges of working with the public, reading for groups of people and the rigors that this work entails. I was a new talent on the scene and working very hard to establish my legitimacy and credibility. It was a difficult time for me that was often draining and discouraging, as I fought to prove myself and the value of my work. There were many times when I was starting out, that I felt dispirited and discouraged. Alan befriended me and took me under his wing. He was always a phone call away with plenty of advice, encouragement and support. Alan's words would lift me up and remind me how important our work really was and why we worked so hard to do what we did. Alan was the one person that I trusted and that I could talk to who knew exactly what I was going through.

On the morning just after his passing, I had just finished some early morning readings at my office, and while checking my messages on the way home in the car, I got a voicemail from a friend asking if I'd heard about Alan. I listened to the message as I unlocked the front door to my home. I initially assumed from the message that Alan must be sick or maybe in the hospital, until I opened the door and saw him in spirit standing in my living room. Alan had been living with Muscular Dystrophy for years and had recently confided to me that he believed it was getting worse and that his time here was winding down. He had been writing his book at the time and was anxious to get it finished feeling his time was coming to a close.

Tears began streaming down my face as I began to digest the unexpected news and I cried "No!"

In a very familiar deep voice that I could hear as clearly as if he were talking to me on the phone, he said "Hey Denise, its Alan," He was beaming and had a big grin on his face. "I died last night in my sleep."

"Alan, No! I'm not ready for you to go. I need you here, I still need you." I cried.

He was laughing cheerfully as he said, "Why are you crying? You know where I am. I'm standing right here," and he seemed genuinely puzzled by my emotional reaction.

"I know Alan but it's not the same, I'm not ready for you to go yet. It's too soon."

Still smiling and laughing, as he always did, he said, "Well I'm done here and I've stayed long enough to train my replacement," and I knew he meant me.

"I just came by to say good bye before I go."

I could tell he was so happy to finally be free of the limitations of his physical body that had become so crippling in his last years. He told me how he was enjoying going all over the place and visiting people and I knew he was making his rounds before he went home. He hung out with me again for a short time the next day to watch one of my readings. He asked if I minded if he watched my reading and told me that he wanted to see what the process of communicating with us was like now from the spirits point of view.

Then he came to me once more the next night, before he crossed over and went home.

He was actually quite distraught this time as he told me that he was very upset that his wife was so devastated and not taking his death very well. He was frustrated that he could not get through to her and comfort her because of her intense grief. He expressed to me how difficult it was for him to be on the other side of things and no longer be able to offer comfort to his wife, when he had spent his lifetime providing it for so many others. He asked me to deliver a brief message to his wife, which I left on her answering machine the next day. It was the last time I saw Alan on this side of life before he crossed over and went home to the spirit side. Before he left, the last thing he said to me was in regard to his wife. I will never forget Alan's words…

"I never knew it would be so hard to say good bye."

–And as it is so hard to say good bye, not only for us, but for our loved one's going home, is why sometimes they work so hard to get through to us–just one last time.

"And as it is, so hard to say good-bye, is why…
I am their Messenger."

Denise Lescano is a world renowned Professional Spirit Medium, Intuitive Consultant, Metaphysical Teacher and Author. She is well known and widely respected, for the groundbreaking and unprecedented work that she does with non-profit Grief Support and Addiction Recovery groups. She specializes in working with those who have lost loved ones by sudden or accidental death and suicide. Denise is recognized and sought after for her highly developed intuitive gifts and her ability to deliver very detailed, personal and evidential messages from loved ones on the spirit side of life. Her penetrating insight and abilities are like no other. She teaches seminars and reads for clients all over the world and maintains an office in Naples, FL, where she resides with her family. For more information about Denise and her work, please visit ...

www.deniselescano.com

www.ingramcontent.com/pod-product-compliance
Lightning Source LLC
Chambersburg PA
CBHW051755040426
42446CB00007B/379